Praise

'This book
a 'real-life'
right start
siasm and

'I lost cou
knew that
book. It i
would-be
established
murky woi
peoples' id
all these ar
teachers pa
tion period

'It is every
keep by your side when the going gets tough (which it invariably
does) and a guiding vo
get all my student tea
will find it superbly he

'A great guide for teaching practice and the first year answering a
lot of the questions which lectures and being in the classroom
don't, as well as giving the reality of the role in plain E

J

Other titles in the *Brilliant Teacher* series:

trainee teacher

What you need to know to be a truly outstanding teacher

Denise Smith

Prentice Hall
is an imprint of

Harlow, England • London • New York • Boston • San Francisco • Toronto • Sydney • Singapore • Hong Kong
Tokyo • Seoul • Taipei • New Delhi • Cape Town • Madrid • Mexico City • Amsterdam • Munich • Paris • Milan

PEARSON EDUCATION LIMITED

Edinburgh Gate
Harlow CM20 2JE
Tel: +44 (0)1279 623623
Fax: +44 (0)1279 431059
Website: www.pearsoned.co.uk

First published in Great Britain in 2011

© Pearson Education 2011

The right of Denise Smith to be identified as author of this work has been
asserted by her in accordance with the Copyright, Designs and Patents Act
1988.

ISBN: 978-0-273-73246-4

British Library Cataloguing-in-Publication Data
A catalogue record for this book is available from the British Library

Library of Congress Cataloging-in-Publication Data
Smith, Denise.
    Brilliant trainee teacher / Denise Smith.
        p. cm. -- (Brilliant teacher series)
    Includes index.
    ISBN 978-0-273-73246-4 (pbk.)
    1. Effective teaching. 2. Teachers--Training of. 3. First year teachers. I. Title.
    LB1025.3.S62 2011
    371.102--dc22
                                    2010049716

10 9 8 7 6 5 4 3 2 1
15 14 13 12 11

Typeset in 10/14pt Plantin by 3
Printed in Great Britain by Henry Ling Ltd, at the Dorset Press, Dorchester,
Dorset

To Martin Rees

I couldn't have asked for a wiser, more patient and supportive mentor

Contents

Foreword

I taught for 14 years in three different schools before anyone came to observe one of my lessons. There was an assumption that you were somehow born a teacher, and you could somehow pick up whatever skills you had failed to inherit in your genes.

Thank goodness it's different now. As a result of research, professional learning amongst teachers and advances in neuroscience, we now have a vastly improved understanding of how children learn and so how good teachers should teach. We understand that teaching is both a profession and a craft, the sum of all our formative experiences and of skills that we can learn, practise and improve.

We also increasingly appreciate that the quality of teaching is the most important factor in driving the performance of students. Research by Sanders and Rivers (1996) in Tennessee dramatically proved the point. Take two students at the 50th percentile who go to the same school, with the same books, the same curriculum, the same resources, the same everything. Except one has a good teacher, one a bad. In three years their performance will diverge by 53 percentage points. If they start at the 50th percentile, the one with the good teacher will be at the 90th percentile, the one with the bad at the 37th percentile.

There can be no better justification for this book. It exudes the inspiration, enthusiasm and moral purpose you need to be a professional. It gives you a wealth of brilliant, practical tips to develop your craft. You could ask for no better start to your career as a brilliant teacher.

Roger Pope, Principal, Kingsbridge Community College

About the author

Denise Smith is in her eighth year of teaching Science. She has an honours degree in Biology and did her PGCE in Science at Oxford University. During her NQT year in Bicester, she entered the Fast Track Teaching programme, designed to provide more professional development than is otherwise ordinarily available and to get the teacher involved in wider school issues. During her fourth year of teaching, she was accredited with the Advanced Skills Teacher status. She thoroughly enjoys her job and has said that she would only leave teaching if Kate Humble's job became available!

Acknowledgements

I would like to thank Jane McNicholl and Ann Childs from the Oxford University Department of Education. They taught us trainees brilliantly, were highly inspiring and gave us lots of ideas on how to make a lesson interesting for our pupils. They were positive throughout and made us really enjoy teaching. My thanks for that year also go out to the Science staff at The Cooper School in Bicester, who were constantly encouraging towards me and were great role models, with an excellent rapport with the pupils.

I would like to thank Gareth Davies, the Headteacher of my previous school, for all of the support he gave me in my professional development. Gareth really encouraged me to be the best teacher that I can be. I am also very grateful to Gill Battye, the Principal of my current school for her faith, constant support generally, and her enthusiasm towards this book.

I couldn't have written this book without the help of my Aunt Sylvia and my Uncle Mike. When I was at school and university, I found writing quite difficult. I have worked hard on gaining the skills, but before I sent my first version to Pearson Education, I got Sylvia and Mike to check it for me. Their feedback built my confidence enough actually to send it off. Sylvia has been of so much support in many different ways throughout my life and is a big inspiration to me.

I am indebted to the editor from Pearson Education, Katy Robinson, for her positive and constructive feedback and for her patience. She has been a joy to work with.

Finally, I would like to thank my ever-supportive husband Dan, who does very well in suppressing his 'Oh, what is she doing now?' thoughts whenever I come up with a new idea, like writing a book. After taking the opportunity to internalise it for a few seconds, he always looks for the benefit and offers to help in whatever way he can. Thank you.

Publisher's acknowledgements

We are grateful to the following for permission to reproduce copyright material:

Appendix 1 from the Training and Development Agency website (www.tda.gov.uk) © TDA 2010. Reproduced with permission from the Training and Development Agency for Schools. Appendix 3 adapted from Rogers, *You Know the Fair Rule: Strategies for Making the Hard Job of Discipline in Schools Easier*, Financial Times Prentice Hall, 1998. Reproduced with permission of the author.

In some instances we have been unable to trace the owners of copyright material, and we would appreciate any information that would enable us to do so.

Introduction

I'm not a morning person, but I have to get up at half past six every day. I have a long journey and a very early meeting and then, by half past eight, I'm wide awake, in a room with 30 teenagers. Suddenly, I have forgotten how early the alarm clock went off and I am in a place full of excitement and energy.

Teaching is a highly rewarding career. I love my subject and I am in the extremely privileged position of being able to share it with others. When I am teaching and a pupil says 'Oh right!' in realisation, or from those more subtle I see a raise of the eyebrows and a nod, it evokes an internal smile. I sometimes even get a 'No way! Can we do that again?' when they are conducting a scientific experiment. Then, a pupil who has been sitting quietly will ask a question that makes me realise that they have been thinking really deeply about the topic and are intrigued to find out more.

I have regular discussions in the staff room that include predicting who will become a scientist. Of course, other teachers often disagree and think that same pupil has great prospects in a different career. But the thought that I might have inspired somebody so much that they want to learn more is encouragement enough to continue planning stimulating lessons. I am having an impact on the next generation. I might be teaching my pupils things that they will teach their children in the future. I might be rousing lifelong hobbies.

In addition, we teachers have a responsibility to pass on life skills. We must challenge our pupils to become kind, patient, perseverant, generous and curious. We will watch some of our pupils become the leaders and the carers of the future. And then, at the end of our time with them, it's results day. I am able to watch pupils' eyes light up when they see their grades and observe them proudly telling people their achievements. I have a part in that. I have a part in providing these pupils with choices about how they wish to lead their lives.

Teaching is a job in which I can exhibit creativity. It is a job in which I can meet a huge variety of characters and laugh with them every day. I have learned a massive number of skills, ranging from organisational to interpersonal, all of which I will carry with me throughout the rest of my life, in all parts of it. I cannot imagine a more challenging or stimulating career. It also comes with many perks, such as the holidays, which tie in very well with families, and the security. There will always be a need for teachers! So why is teaching not always seen to be an attractive career choice?

'Those that can't, teach.'

'I don't know how you could work with people of that age.'

'The teacher training year is the hardest year of your life.'

'The first year of qualified teaching is the hardest of your life.'

I had heard all of these. So, it is perhaps not surprising that I cried when I realised that I was going to have to do my Post Graduate Certificate in Education (PGCE). I had just received a letter telling me that I hadn't got the job that I had recently been interviewed for in wildlife education. I had been working for the Wildlife Trust and had been doing a good job, but had been told that if I wanted to progress my career in teaching about wildlife, then I had to get a PGCE.

Well, I thought I should just grit my teeth and get on with it. When I went for my interview for the course, so many images from when I was at school sprang to mind: pupils swearing at teachers; throwing things; locking teachers in cupboards and jumping in and out of windows. I absolutely winged the interview, saying how much I really wanted to be a teacher and so on. I'm so glad that they believed me!

Some of these nightmare images have happened, but thankfully I have avoided the missiles and have not been taken prisoner (but to be frank, you're kind of asking for it, if you walk inside a cupboard with a key in the door in a room full of teenagers!). What I came to realise is that when you understand pupils' motivations and what they need from their teachers, it doesn't make bad behaviour on their part acceptable, but it means that you don't have to go home worrying about it, or about the nature of society these days. It also means that you can forgive more easily and use the experience to build a better relationship with them. The proof that I love the job is that I'm still in it.

Teaching is an immense challenge, though it's not as hard as people make it out to be. However, it does require a lot of time. If you're prepared to put the time in, without resenting it, and have a mind that can cope with thinking about many things at once, the rewards really make it worthwhile.

I don't want to sound nauseatingly positive, but I guess you really have to like your job to want to write a book about it. However, I have not written this book as though it's all easy and it addresses many of the challenges likely to be encountered while teaching.

Why read this book?

This book has been written for those people who are thinking of going into teaching and those who are in or about to embark upon their training year. When I was training, I was unable to find any books to guide me through the training course, giving tips on how to cope with the challenges that trainee teachers face and, just as importantly, covering teaching methods, to encourage me to excel in my first year and deliver lessons of an excellent quality. When I noticed that this was still the case, I thought that maybe I should write one. This book will also be useful for those who are already in the career, but would like some further help on the techniques that can be used to deliver an effective, enjoyable lesson. I have written it in a style that will allow the reader to read only the sections they need to at that moment in time, rather than having to read the entire book in one sitting. I know how busy you people are going to be!

For ease of reading, I have left out some detail intentionally. For example, though I have mentioned generally accepted ideas about teaching, I have not gone into detail about the research that was necessary to support these ideas, or about psychological theories. I trust that if you would like some more information, you will find Appendix 5 useful.

Teaching is not, as is believed by some, a way of life. Those people who think it is, I'm afraid, have got the balance wrong. Some teachers work way too hard and – dare I say it – inefficiently. I hope that the following chapters will be useful in ensuring that you become one of the efficient ones!

If you are thinking of undertaking a teacher training course

There are a number of things that I would advise you to consider before you decide to apply for teacher training courses:

● They can be quite intense. All of the tasks given to you during your course will need to be completed. Lessons will need to be planned and resources will need to be made in advance. You will need to be self-disciplined throughout this time because, for example, you cannot arrive at lessons late, leaving a class of 30 pupils waiting for you.

● During those times when you are planning and teaching lots of lessons, while you are building up a bank of ideas and resources, you will need to work on some evenings and weekends. This can be quite tiring and may require you to think about, for example, childcare arrangements.

● It is a highly rewarding time and you will gain skills rapidly. Learning these skills will require a lot of energy, but they can be drawn upon for the rest of your life.

● Teaching is an excellent career for people with young children or for those who think they might have a family in the future. The timings of the day and the holidays allow teachers to spend more time with their children than many other full-time careers.

● You are likely to meet lots of people who will be able to help you, including fellow students. It's great to share ideas with people in a similar position.

Tips to help you make your decision

If you are not sure whether teaching is the career for you, the following suggestions will help you to decide:

● Talk to some teachers. If any of your friends, family or acquaintances are teachers, ask them to give you an honest breakdown of the advantages and disadvantages of the job.

● Gain some work experience. Ask if you could help out at a local school for a few days to observe what teaching really involves and practise working with pupils of your chosen age.

Finally, good luck and I hope this book proves to be useful in helping you to become a successful teacher.

PART 1

Starting out

CHAPTER 1

How to get into teaching

I t was Henry Adams who said that 'A teacher affects eternity; he can never tell where his influence stops' (Adams and Nadel, 2008). That's quite a scary thought! But in reality, it *is* why we become teachers. Teaching is certainly a job in which you really can make a difference, possibly to thousands of people. So, the people responsible for choosing who gets onto their teacher training course need to make sure they find people with the ability to do this. This chapter will provide tips on how to demonstrate that you are one of those people. Firstly, though, we will look at the different types of courses available to you.

Please note that there are many references to websites throughout the rest of this chapter. You will find the web addresses in Appendix 4. Teaching is a profession riddled with acronyms. If you come across an acronym and can't remember what it stands for, please refer to Appendix 6.

Which course?

To be able to gain Qualified Teacher Status (QTS), it is essential that you complete an Initial Teacher Training (ITT) programme. There are a variety of such courses, depending on your qualifications, teaching experience, income requirements, time available and aspirations. These courses are outlined in Appendix 1. Please note that as well as the qualification requirements in Appendix 1, individual training providers may have their own requirements, which will be detailed during the application procedure. If you have gained qualifications in other countries, you can find out if they are equivalent to the requirements of these courses by visiting the website of the UK National Academic Recognition Information Centre. The web address is in Appendix 4.

Below is a bit more detail about the structure of the courses, but first, there are some general aspects that are applicable to all of them. Please note that all of the lengths given are on a full-time basis, but many providers offer their courses on a part-time basis also. If you already have some undergraduate credits, you may be able to complete the course in a shorter amount of time. It is wise, in this situation, to contact the course provider before you apply. It is also worth bearing in mind that all jobs that involve working with children involve a compulsory Criminal Records Bureau (CRB) check.

your teaching experience will increase throughout the programme

In all teaching courses, your teaching experience will increase throughout the programme. You will begin by observing lessons delivered by other teachers. The next step varies, depending on the teacher or the school. You will be asked either to start working with small groups of pupils, or to take small sections of lessons or to team teach. That is, you will teach alongside the class teacher and you will help each other. Then, you will start to teach full lessons. Eventually, you will probably be asked to take all of the lessons of particular classes. Some teachers might, when they have developed the confidence to do so, leave you alone with the class, to retreat to a back room or very close office. You may or may not feel more relaxed without the thought of the teacher watching your every move. However, if you are not comfortable with it, you are perfectly within your rights to ask them to stay in the lessons and conversely, do not be offended if they don't leave. Some teachers will never leave a trainee teacher alone with a class. After all, although it is imperative that you behave as professionally as a qualified teacher, the safety of the pupils and their education remains the responsibility of the normal teacher throughout your training year.

To coincide with this structure of increasing lengths of time spent teaching and with increasing frequency, your time in school will increase throughout most courses.

> your time in school will increase throughout most courses

At the start of the course, you will receive a lot of training about teaching issues and strategies, subject knowledge and how to deliver effective lessons. You will have the chance to ask questions and work with other trainees. The balance of training and teaching shifts throughout the programme as the teaching load increases.

The decision to award you with QTS at the end of your teaching course will lie with different people, depending on the course. The class teachers will be required to assess and evaluate your lessons, producing forms containing a summary. You will use these forms as evidence of what you have achieved. They will need to tell you what went well and what they recommend you work on, to ensure that you are meeting the QTS Standards, a set of statements describing what a trainee teacher needs to be able to do, in order to pass their training year. If you would like to view the Standards in advance, visit the Training and Development Agency for Schools (TDA) website (Appendix 4).

Towards the end of the course, the person responsible will start to observe full lessons to assess your ability to teach. Often, if you haven't quite passed yet, you will be told on which of the Standards you need to work and you will be given further opportunities.

In addition to your teaching practice, most courses will also require you to

> most courses will also require you to conduct research in schools

conduct research in schools, in order to complete school-based assignments. These will be about current teaching issues and how they affect education. There is a section providing guidance on school-based assignments in Chapter 3.

Another requirement before you can achieve QTS is to pass three computer-based exams, covering Numeracy, Literacy and ICT. These have been made compulsory by the government to ensure teachers themselves have a certain standard of education. These are called QTS tests and are covered in more detail in Chapter 3.

When you gain QTS, you will be legally allowed to teach anywhere in the UK. Of course, if ever you did want to teach abroad, the skills learned are recognised as being highly transfer-rable and teachers are one of the few groups of people that many countries are actively seeking. However, to be concise and for clarity, this book will refer to teaching within the UK.

Key Stages

Key Stages are mentioned quite a lot in the next few sections. A Key Stage is a stage of education, largely based on the age of the child. Here is a guide:

- Early Years – birth to 5
- Key Stage 1 – ages 5–7
- Key Stage 2 – ages 7–11
- Key Stage 3 – ages 11–14
- Key Stage 4 – ages 14–16
- Key Stage 5 – often ages 16–18, but mature pupils are able to study at this level in many schools.

The 'primary level' includes Key Stages 1–2, although many primary schools offer 'Early Years' education. The 'secondary level' includes Key Stages 3–4, with many secondary schools also offering Key Stage 5 education.

For all of the courses outlined below, consult the TDA website (Appendix 4) to find suitable training providers. It contains a comparison activity that will allow you to choose your course based on one or more of the following: postcode, provider, subject, region and TDA quality category.

brilliant tip

It is worth investing a good deal of time investigating the most appropriate pathway into teaching for you. Your choice of course could really affect your enjoyment and success. Feel free to phone course providers with any questions you might have.

Bachelor of Education (BEd)

This is the course you may choose to do if you know you definitely want to become a teacher. It is usually a four-year course, and will leave you with an honours degree in Education and Qualified Teacher Status (QTS). The two qualifications are studied together, as part of the same course.

This course is particularly good if you wish to teach primary-aged pupils, as you will be required to teach a variety of different subjects, each of which will be studied. The course is also available to you if you would like to become a secondary teacher, but because secondary teaching is usually specific to one subject, it may be best for you to complete a standard honours degree in a chosen subject and then complete a course such as the PGCE (see page 11). This would leave you with more options, if you were to decide to change career at any point in the future.

The BEd course begins in the first year with general studies of aspects of teaching, such as assessment (see Chapter 8), lesson planning (Chapter 11) and behaviour management (Chapter 13). It will also involve some time in school.

Your experience in schools will increase in length and involvement in lessons throughout the next three years. You will spend time in a different school each year and will probably spend some time in a school specifically for pupils with Special Educational Needs (SEN). The experience will be sure to cover at least two Key Stages.

In the final two years, on the primary course, you will be asked to choose which Key Stage (Early Years, 1 or 2) you would prefer to specialise in and further studies will be planned around this choice. This does not apply to you if you wish to teach at the secondary level, because you may be required to teach all Key Stages – 3, 4 and 5.

Also in the second half of the course, you will be asked to choose your subject specialism, for example Humanities, English, Mathematics, Science or Music. You will thereafter study some modules specific to that specialism. Many of these courses contain some form of examination, whether multiple choice or written, in Mathematics, English and ICT, plus the specialism subject if different. In addition to this, you must also pass the compulsory QTS tests.

At the end of this course, if successful, you will gain two qualifications: the degree qualification, based on all aspects of your studies; and your education qualification, based on your teaching alone. The two grades awarded are not always the same.

Training for a Bachelor of Arts (BA) or a Bachelor of Science (BSc) degree, alongside achieving QTS

If you would like to gain a degree about a specific subject, i.e. not in general education, and become a teacher at the same time, this could be the course for you. At the end of it, if successful, you will have the degree of your choice, plus the QTS status.

This course is not similar to the BEd course above, because your degree is separate from the teaching qualification, which actually means that you are not tied in to teaching and could use the degree for many other occupations. It is therefore more appropriate for secondary teachers, who require a degree-level subject specialism anyway. This route is actually very similar to gaining a degree and then completing a PGCE (see below), but the teaching qualification is undertaken at the same time as the degree, rather than afterwards. It is worth noting here that your independent degree will involve examinations and probably a dissertation. Your teaching will also be formally assessed during the final year by observations of your lessons. This could make your final year quite intense.

Post Graduate Certificate in Education or Professional Graduate Certificate in Education (both known as the PGCE)

If you already have a degree, this year-long course is a good option. It covers teaching strategies and theories outlined in the introduction to the courses above and if successful, you will gain QTS status and a PGCE. You could also work towards a Masters in Teaching and Learning (MTL – see the TDA website for further information), which will be completed once you have qualified.

The difference between the Post Graduate Certificate in Education and the Professional Graduate Certificate in Education is that the former is achieved if you have gained 60 masters credits. The latter is the title you will hold if you have passed the course, but have achieved fewer than 60 masters credits.

Most PGCE courses begin with some time each week in college or university, where the bulk of the training sessions are delivered, and some time in school. Towards the end of the course, you will probably be spending all of your time in school. The person who undertakes your final assessments is likely to be a university or college representative familiar to you. The PGCE is suitable for both primary and secondary teaching and will include experience of at least two different schools.

School-centred Initial Teacher Training (SCITT)

If you wish to spend more time in schools than the other courses offer, this is likely to be the most appropriate course. It differs from the PGCE in that SCITT pupils are based mainly in the school from the start of the year. The school will be working with other schools in the area to provide this course, so you may be required to spend some time in other schools, too.

The SCITT course is overseen by a university, but most of the assessment will be implemented by teachers within the school. Many SCITT courses will leave you with a PGCE as well as QTS status, but you will need to check this before you apply, because it is not always the case.

Please note that there are currently no SCITT courses running in Wales alone, but there are some that involve a school in Wales and a school in England.

 **brilliant** tip

> For the most up-to-date information on the courses available, go to the TDA website, listed in Appendix 4.

Graduate Teacher Programme (GTP)

In this course, you will learn to teach 'on the job'. It is suitable for you if you have some experience of teaching, or a related discipline, and need to be paid a salary (an unqualified teacher's salary – see the TES website (Appendix 4) for an up-to-date idea of the value of this). You will be required to gain experience in two different schools and at two different Key Stages. Alongside the lessons, you are given training, which is designed to suit your individual needs. You will be expected to have some input to the design of your own training programme.

Owing to the requirement of previous experience, progress on this course is expected to be quicker than on other courses. For example, there is less time spent observing other teachers and you will be delivering more full lessons, at an earlier stage.

Registered teacher programme

If you have at least two years' experience in higher education, but haven't quite got a degree (so, maybe an HND), but you do have some experience in teaching or a related area, this may be the course that will best meet your requirements. In this two-year course, you will be able to extend your subject knowledge to degree level and if successful, you will be awarded that degree. You will also gain QTS status. Teaching experience is required, as this, like the GTP programme above, involves teaching full lessons at an earlier stage. As a result, you will receive an unqualified teacher's salary (see the TES website).

You will spend around 80 per cent of your time in school and around 20 per cent of your time in the university, working towards your degree, which will either be in Education or a specific subject, appropriate for secondary teaching. As with the GTP programme, you will receive school-based training about teaching issues and methods, which will be tailored to suit your individual needs.

Teach First

If you already have a degree and know that you have aspirations of becoming part of the Senior Leadership Team (SLT, which includes Assistant Headteachers, Deputy Headteachers and Headteachers), or holding another leadership position within education, this could be the course in which you progress the fastest. That is not to say, however, that taking one of the other courses means that you won't be able to do that. It's just that this is the only teacher training course that provides specific leadership training.

Teach First is a highly selective course, requiring at least a 2:1 degree, and has a rigorous selection procedure. It also differs from other routes into teaching in that it deliberately places you into two challenging schools. It pays you an unqualified teacher's salary in the first year (see the TES website) and a Newly Qualified Teacher (NQT) salary in the second year.

brilliant tip

At the end of the 2009–2010 academic year, the Teach First programme had been looking to expand the number of schools and areas in which teachers can complete this course. Check their website (Appendix 4) for the most up-to-date information.

Assessment-based training

If you already have experience in teaching, but do not have QTS, for example if you have been working as an unqualified teacher, you can submit evidence of your ability to teach, to be able to achieve QTS. You will then undergo a one-day assessment in your school by an outside assessor. This could result in you gaining QTS in a much shorter period of time than if you were to undertake one of the above courses.

Please note that there are similar teacher training courses running in Scotland. For more information on training to teach in Scotland, please go to www.teachinginscotland.com.

Funding

The funding you are eligible to receive will depend on the course you choose, the subject you are training to teach or specialise in and your personal circumstances. Table 1.1 is a summary of the different funding options available.

*Please note that for information on the funding available to people
training to teach in Scotland, please visit www.teachinginscotland.
com.*

 **tip**

To find out which of these funding options you are eligible for, go
to the Direct.gov website, listed in Appendix 4.

Course	Funding available (depending on eligibility)	
	England	Wales
BEd, BA with QTS and BSc with QTS	Tuition fee loans Maintenance loans Maintenance grant	Grant for school-based placement*
PGCE and SCITT	Tuition fee loan Tax-free training bursary* 'Golden hello' when you have completed your NQT year*	Tax-free bursary* Teaching grant when you have completed your NQT year* Welsh medium improvement supplement, if you are training through the medium of Welsh.
GTP and RTP	At least the minimum point on the unqualified teacher's pay scale.	At least the minimum point on the unqualified teacher's pay scale. RTP not available in Wales.
Teach First	Depends on area. Contact Teach First.	Not currently available in Wales.

* depending on the subject you are training to teach or specialise in.

Table 1.1 Funding available for pupils undertaking teacher training courses
(Information correct at the time of press. Check the TDA website for the most
up-to-date information.)

Gain experience in schools before you apply

I cannot recommend this enough. It could really help you gain an understanding of the workings of a school and give you the opportunity to see how others interact with pupils and encourage them to learn. It will also impress interviewers from training institutions!

Volunteering in schools

There are a number of ways in which you could gain experience. You could ask to volunteer in a school, which would allow you some flexibility. Unfortunately though, schools are more reluctant to ask for people to come in to help these days because they must make sure every adult working with their pupils has been CRB checked. This process can take a number of weeks. There are more formal and well-recognised ways of gaining experience, such as the Student Associates Scheme (SAS) and working as a Teaching Assistant (TA).

Student Associates Scheme

This scheme involves some induction and training, followed by three weeks spent in a school, working with the members of staff to assist in the education of their pupils. Because they know that the reason you are doing this is probably to build a foundation for your teacher training, the teachers will help you by explaining what they're doing and involving you in the process. There is a daily tax-free bursary for people undertaking this scheme. To find a list of schools in which the SAS takes place, visit the TDA website.

Working as a TA

An option that suited me better was working as a Teaching Assistant (TA). There are often such posts advertised in the local newspapers and they involve working with SEN pupils – those who need a bit more help to be able to achieve their potential. See Chapter 9 for more information. Working as a TA can be quite demanding as it requires a lot of patience and energy, but it is highly rewarding. You may be asked to work on a one-to-one basis with a pupil, or as a general assistant to the class teacher. This role will give you an excellent insight into the pupils' needs, which will make you a better teacher. You will be paid for your work, although the salary is not high.

brilliant tip

There are several courses available for those wishing to increase their chances of gaining a TA post, and for providing them with a foundation of understanding for the role. I have never found this to be necessary for actually getting a job, but if your experience suggests it would be a good idea, find the courses by typing something like 'preparing to become a Teaching Assistant' into a search engine.

If you do wish to apply for a TA post, when writing your letter to the Headteacher, make sure you convey professionalism, enthusiasm and commitment to education. Write why you think you are suitable for the job, by including the valuable skills you have. For more tips on your application, many of the aspects of applying for a teaching course will apply to this situation too.

brilliant tip

Do not refrain from writing in your letter that you wish to gain experience before you apply to become a teacher. That will make it clear that you will work hard while you are there.

Other educational roles

Other appropriate forms of experience include any other job working in the education of young people. It could be that you work in a theatre group with school pupils, or for an environmental organisation. You might take exchange pupils on excursions. A job from which you could receive a good reference about your ability to relate to pupils or to inspire young people in your preferred subject or specialism will be advantageous.

brilliant tip

If you are able to get some experience in working with children, ensure before you leave that you ask somebody personally (preferably the Headteacher, if it's a school) to be your referee. It will encourage them to start to make mental notes.

Your application

When you are filling in your teacher training application, you will have to complete a written section, often called the Personal Statement, to communicate why you think you should be accepted onto the course. Even if the following questions aren't outlined, they should be answered as part of your statement:

● Why do you want to be a teacher?
  - Is it a lifelong ambition?
  - Did a certain job or something happen to make you realise that it was a career you wanted to embark upon?
● What have you done to pursue this?
  - Outline any experience you have had.
    - Work experience at a school?
    - Volunteer work with children?
    - Other work in your subject's field?

Write some examples of things you have learned from this experience to demonstrate its value, for example:

- Did you learn always to keep a calm voice?
- Did you learn the importance of restating instructions?
- Did you learn the value of patience for creating a positive learning environment?

● How is your education relevant to becoming a teacher?

- Do your qualifications directly tie in with the National Curriculum subject you are applying to teach?
- If you are teaching at the primary level, mention your Mathematics, English and Science qualifications and how you are looking forward to teaching them.
- Do you have any other qualifications that are in any way relevant?

  I even mentioned a minor qualification I had in teaching badminton. Anything extra like this helps to show that you are an active, enthusiastic person who seizes opportunities.

● What skills do you have that will help you to do your job as a teacher well?

- Relate them to specific parts of the teaching job, for example:
  - Are you organised?

    If you meet deadlines well, it will enable you to mark books, plan lessons and put in any resource orders on time.

  - Are you punctual?

    This means that you will ensure you are at lessons and meetings on time.

  - Do you work well as part of a team?

    If you do, it means you will be able to take advice and share experience and resources.

- Are you able to work independently?

  If so, it will mean that you will seek advice when necessary, but you will also be able to work creatively, injecting your own ideas into your lesson planning.

- Are you enthusiastic?

  This means that you will convey your lessons with energy, which will inspire the pupils.

- Do you have good computer skills?

  If you do, it will allow you to be efficient and organised. It will also mean that you will use e-learning (Chapter 10) effectively in your lessons.

● Mention some aspects of your personality that will ensure you make a good teacher.

  - Are you committed to the education of young people? Why?

  - Are there any other hobbies or other experiences that demonstrate that you are self-disciplined (such as a martial art, or the completion of the Duke of Edinburgh Award), thorough (photography?), proactive (were you once in the School Council?) or able to commit to things (are you a part-time instructor in any other field, or do you volunteer for charities?)?

  - Is there anything else that will make you stand out?

● Why have you chosen this particular course?

  - Have you read about any of the statistics or know of its high quality?

  - Is there something about the structure of the course that makes it particularly suitable?

When writing your application, start with those facts that are most relevant to the teaching of your subject or desired specialism. Make sure you don't exceed the word or line limit, especially if it's an online application, because they won't be able to read the end. It is very important that you do not exaggerate anything so much that it actually becomes untrue! That is likely to be the thing that they ask you about, if it sounds particularly special.

brilliant tip

Remember to get somebody else to check your application for you. Even if your spelling and grammar are excellent, when you have read something over and over again, you may well keep missing the mistake, just through familiarity. Also try actually reading your text out loud to yourself. Oh, and don't rely on the computer's spellchecker!

The interview

Before your interview, I would recommend that you research the structure of the course, so you know exactly how much of the course is school based and how much is college or university based and so on. The interviewers will not want to see an expression of surprise in response to any of their comments. There are certain personality traits the interviewers will be looking for. A few of these are:

● enthusiasm;

● dedication;

● commitment;

● love for your subject or specialism;

● appreciation for the value of education;

● responsibility (so it is possible to trust the safety of pupils in your care);

● an eagerness to learn;

● respect for the role of teachers.

Secondly, they will be trying to find out if you know much about teaching. They may ask you how you feel about certain issues facing teachers. To prepare yourself for this, I would recommend that you buy a current newspaper or magazine dedicated to teaching, to be able to read up on such matters before the interview. Of course, another reason for gaining experience in a school beforehand is that you will be aware of teaching issues already and will be able to talk about them in a way that shows you really believe and understand what you say.

Current hot topics

Here is a list of things that I recommend you research before your interview. They are seen as very important documents or issues in educational institutions:

- **Assessment for Learning/Assessing Pupil Progress** – see Chapter 8.

- **Behaviour Management** – see Chapter 13.

- **E-learning** – see Chapter 10.

- **Every Child Matters/Duty of Care/Safeguarding** – Every Child Matters is the Government's initiative to make learning accessible to all, regardless of circumstances. It also ensures that all organisations involved in pupil welfare work together to ensure pupils are safe and healthy – see the website in Appendix 4.

- **The National Curriculum** – the documents that tell teachers exactly what must be taught to pupils – see the website in Appendix 4.

- **The National Strategies** – ways of making learning and progression more engaging and accessible to students – see the website in Appendix 4.

- **SEN/Inclusion/Meeting Individual Needs/ Differentiation/Gifted and Talented/Group Work** – see Chapter 9.

- **Student/Pupil Voice** – the drive for schools to take the opinions of their pupils into account when planning new developments in education. It involves, for example, meetings with pupils and asking them to complete questionnaires about the school.
- **VAK/Learning Styles** – see Chapter 7.

brilliant tip

Gain an understanding of the course provider's priorities by reading the prospectus. For example, if they mention 'a passion for education' many times, make sure you slip it in during the interview.

The formality of the interview will depend on the course providers. They may wish to have more of a chat than a question and answer session. However, it is always a good idea to dress smartly, so it is clear that you would be prepared to dress professionally during your school placement. The format of the session or day varies between providers. Some will conduct interviews one candidate at a time, but some will hold them on a group basis, where they will also be looking for your ability to work with others. Here, you would have to show that you are able to wait your turn, but are assertive enough to ensure that you do have a turn. You would need to show that you are able to listen to the other interviewees' comments and respond to them in a positive, constructive way. Your interview might involve a task of some kind, about which you will probably be notified in advance. You might be taken on a campus tour.

brilliant tip

If you are required to give a presentation, phone the number on the letter inviting you to interview to ask what resources they have available. For example, you cannot guarantee the availability of a projector. Remember to show off other creative and interactive skills as well as your ICT skills.

The interviewers will be looking for you to speak clearly and not too rushed. They will look for you to speak with commitment. The reason they will be looking for these skills is that they are required for you to be able to communicate effectively with pupils.

If you arrive on time, well dressed and perhaps with a notebook and pen, it will show that you are organised. It is perfectly acceptable to make notes during an interview, even if it is about a question that you would like to ask. Just ask 'Do you mind if I make a couple of notes, please?' They will have no issue with you consulting some notes you have made. They will also be happy for you to have some questions prepared, as it will show that you have been thinking carefully about what you are applying for.

Here are some examples of the kinds of questions you may be asked during your interview:

- Why do you want to be a teacher?

  Although, sadly, it is some applicants' main reason, make sure you don't say it's because you don't know what else to do. You need to demonstrate a commitment to teaching.

- Why do you want to teach History?

- Tell me what you learned during the Student Associates Scheme.

  Interviewers will be looking for your evaluative skills. Don't be afraid to tell them that you weren't aware that ... [example] before the placement and that it has been very useful. Mention the skills you have developed. Feel free to draw upon certain situations (not mentioning any names) and tell them what you learned from them.

- During your school experience, what teaching techniques or behaviour management techniques did you observe that were particularly effective?
- How would you teach somebody to work out $(-1) + 1$?
- What do you think you would do if a pupil came to you with a problem?

  Here, they might be looking for the fact that you are aware of your limitations. It would be wise to show that you are willing to go to other members of staff for help if you don't know what to do.

- Are there any extra-curricular activities that you would help the school in?

  The answer to this should definitely be 'Yes', but think carefully in advance about what extra-curricular skills you have to offer. They will be impressed to see that you are a well-rounded person with other interests.

- How would you teach ... [here they may insert a topic that should be familiar to you, but that might be deemed to be boring by others] in an exciting way?
- What methods would you use to develop a positive relationship with your pupils?

brilliant dos and don'ts

Do

✔ Do gain as much experience as possible. If you do work in a school, try to get experience of many different areas, so you get a good understanding of how a school works. It also helps to reassure you that it is a good career for you.

✔ Do feel free to contact the course providers with any queries you have about the course. It is important that you have all of the details correct before you commit at least a year of your life to it.

▶

✔ Do think hard about how any skills and experiences you have from previous jobs can be transferred to teaching and how you will communicate this in your application.

✔ Do be honest in your interview. There are plenty of past experiences that will help you with your teaching and ability to relate to pupils and fellow teachers. You don't need to make them up.

✔ Do be familiar with the National Curriculum (and the syllabus if teaching at Key Stage 4 or above). You may be asked to discuss it and it would be a good idea to quote it in a presentation.

✔ Do be aware that everybody you interact with on the day might feed back to the course selectors. Even if you arrive in a real rush, use manners with everybody you speak to and feel free to ask sensible questions of people you meet during the day.

Don't

✘ Don't make out to the interviewers that you're on the pupils' level. Being a mate doesn't make you a strong teacher. They will know that.

 **brilliant** recap

There are many ways to get into teaching, depending on your needs, preferences, experience and qualifications. My recommendations are:

● Gain some experience in teaching before you apply.

● Be careful to choose the course that suits you best.

● Brush up on issues in education and the course itself before you complete your application.

● Think carefully about what will make your application stand out.

● Get someone to help you practise answering questions before the interview.

CHAPTER 2

Experience weeks

You will probably be asked by your training provider to undergo a couple of weeks of school experience, one in a primary school and one in a secondary school. They can be anywhere in the UK. They are important because they will give you an insight into what the pupils have previously experienced or what they will experience, and these weeks will encourage you to develop empathy with them. For example, you may gain an understanding of how frightening it can be for Year 7 pupils to start at a secondary school, because the whole structure of secondary schooling must seem like a different world to them. In addition, it is important to understand the difference in the levels of education and you will learn about the organisation of schools and the procedures used within them.

brilliant tip

Really embed yourself into school life, at both schools, not just the one at the level in which you're planning to teach. Some people make last-minute decisions and decide that they want to teach at a different level from the one they have applied for, after they have spent time in the schools. Universities might accommodate this change of mind and it will be far better for you in the long run to make the choice at this stage. It is actually possible to work as a secondary teacher, for example, if you have a primary teaching qualification, but the job is very different and you may need to complete a conversion course.

It is likely that you will have to organise your own experience weeks. You will be required to write to the school, or arrange a visit to speak to the Headteacher. It is very important to be professional from the outset.

Writing to prospective experience schools

When writing to possible experience schools, find out the name of the Headteacher (you'll find it on the school website) and address the letter directly to them. Introduce yourself by saying why you are writing. Be clear about which course you are doing, when you are starting, when you would be able to complete your experience week and why you have written to this particular school. Include details of any assignments you will be required to complete or state which particular aspects of teaching have been highlighted to you to look out for, so they know what to expect. It would also show that you have put some thought into it.

Below is an example of a letter that could be written to a potential experience school.

brilliant example

Dear [Headteacher's name],

I am about to begin my PGCE Secondary Science course. I will be studying at the [Name of training provider] and the course begins on 19 September 2011.

As part of this course, I am required to gain a week's work experience at a secondary school. I am writing to ask if you would allow me to spend a week in your school. The reason I am writing to you, as Headteacher of [school name], is that I can see from your Ofsted report that your grades are rapidly improving and I would really benefit from observing your teachers. For your perusal, I enclose a copy of the aspects of school life that I am required to observe.

If you were able to accommodate me for a week before this date, I would be most grateful. You are welcome to contact me via e-mail, post or telephone using the above details.

Yours sincerely

✦ brilliant tip

If your efforts appear to have been in vain, there is an open schools programme, operated by The Teaching Information Line, that should be able to help you organise some time in a local school. The telephone number is 0845 6000 991. There is also a school introduction programme, which serves a similar purpose. The telephone number for this is 0845 6000 994. More information about both programmes is available on the TDA website.

During your experience week, you will be asked by your university to explore issues such as how the pupils learn and how the teachers talk to them. You are likely to have to move around the school for a day with a pupil during your secondary placement, to find out what it is like from their perspective. You may find some teachers particularly inspiring. If you do, make some notes (they will expect this) about what they do that engages the pupils so well. You will see that some teachers are particularly effective in controlling behaviour (known as behaviour or classroom management – see Chapter 13). Again, take notes on how they use tone of voice and what kinds of things they say.

you may find some teachers particularly inspiring

You will be expected to help during the lessons. You may be asked to work with particular pupils, some of

you will be expected to help during the lessons

whom might have Special Educational Needs (SEN – Chapter 9). It is valuable to try to identify how these needs affect their ability to complete the work given to them and even how it affects their attitude towards the lesson. An understanding of this will make you a more compassionate teacher. In addition, you will be observing the interaction between teachers, such as the kinds of issues that are discussed in Department meetings and how the teachers work with other members of staff, such as Teaching Assistants and Resource Technicians.

You will spend a large proportion of each experience week observing lessons, which is an unexpectedly tiring experience. It is easy to get the feeling that you're not doing anything under such circumstances, which can make you feel a bit sleepy. It is important, though, to learn as much as you can from these weeks because they are purposeful and will set you up well for your induction week on the new course. During the induction week, you will be asked to raise any issues you encountered in the experience weeks and to discuss certain aspects of the profession.

 **tip**

Aim to impress during your experience weeks – it could make future job applications stand out!

 **examples**

Emily

Emily realised she still hadn't booked her experience weeks. She didn't want to annoy her tutors before she even started the course so she popped into her nearest school to ask if she could do it there. The lady at the desk telephoned the Headteacher, who was busy in a meeting. Emily was asked to wait until the meeting ended.

About half an hour later, after much position adjusting and a few sighs from Emily, the Headteacher came out of her office, with the Local Education Authority (LEA) representative with whom she had been talking. She welcomed Emily, who was wearing jeans and a t-shirt, into her office. Emily explained that she had to get this week of experience done before the course, which starts in a few weeks, and asked if she could do it there, because she's just up the road. The Headteacher wasn't too impressed with the way Emily had conducted herself so far, but because her school worked with Emily's college quite regularly, she agreed to it. She asked Emily to put the request in writing and to be at the school by 8.30am on the first day. Emily thanked the Headteacher and left.

She remembered a few days before the experience was due to begin that she had to put it in writing, so wrote a basic letter, asking if she could do some experience there. On the first day, Emily arrived on time, looking quite smart. She was shown around the room and introduced to the teacher with whom she would spend her first day. Emily sat at the back of the room and watched. After break, she began to get quite tired and started to yawn. The teacher noticed this, but didn't want to say anything.

At the times when the teacher was circulating around the room, Emily watched from where she was at the back of the room. She didn't know if she would be seen as interfering if she went to speak to the pupils.

By lunchtime, Emily felt really tired, partly because she had been sitting at the back of the room not doing very much. The teachers were discussing things she didn't understand, so she just sat quietly. She was relieved when the 3pm bell went, because that meant she could go home. She walked home thinking about how much better it would be when the course did actually begin. She knew that she would be working with pupils she would see on a regular basis and would feel better about walking around and talking to them. 'Never mind,' she thought, 'I'll just get this over and done with.'

At the end of the week, Emily thanked the teacher she was working with and left. Later, when she was in her teaching post, she bumped into those teachers at occasional training sessions, but felt a bit awkward about speaking to them, so she kept her distance.

▶

John

John's experience weeks were very different from Emily's. He wrote formal letters weeks in advance, knowing how short of time Headteachers are. In the letter, he had offered to come in to discuss it if the Headteacher wished, but in the reply he had received, he had been told that was unnecessary. He arrived on time, looking smart, on the first day. Upon introductions, he confidently shook people by the hand and told them he was pleased to meet them. Many of them thought to themselves that his confident manner would really help him to become a good teacher.

When John was told which teacher he would be working with, he approached her in advance and explained an assignment he had to complete about the way teachers ask questions. He asked if it would therefore be OK for him to make notes during the day. Although this did not surprise the teacher, she was grateful that he was polite enough to ask and said it would be fine. John also asked if it would be OK for him to sit with the pupils when they were doing their work and talk to them about their life in school. Again, the teacher gave her permission.

When the teacher was talking, John made notes about how she asked questions. He realised that she always said the name of the child first, before completing her question. He also jotted down some points about the teacher's tone of voice and how she got the pupils' attention if they started to get distracted.

While the pupils were working, John sat on a table and they immediately asked him questions as though he was a familiar member of staff. Some also asked why he was there and he told them that he wanted to see what the lessons were like for pupils in their year. They accepted this reasoning straight away and continued with their work.

At lunchtime, John asked if the teacher said the pupil's name before asking a question deliberately. She was quite impressed that he had noticed and she explained that she felt it gave them a better chance to process the question internally before giving their answer. She continued to ask if he had noticed another pattern of questioning she used and explained all about it. John asked if there were any particular pupils the teacher would like him to work with and she suggested that it would be really useful for him to work with a pupil with special educational needs.

That afternoon, John worked with this pupil. He noticed that because the pupil was having trouble with writing, the work was taking him much longer than the other pupils. Yet, when John spoke to him, he seemed to know all of the answers; he just couldn't get them down on paper. John didn't offer to write for him, because he thought maybe his writing ability would be something the teacher wanted to assess, but he did start to think about things he would do to help this pupil if he was the teacher.

The next day, John was in a lesson that involved the pupils making bread. It was quite a messy job. The poor teacher had pupils calling her over from every corner of the room and was having trouble getting to everyone. So, when he could, John answered the questions. At one point, the teacher looked across at John getting stuck in with the baking and was grateful to have him there.

John had a very successful week at that school. He got on well with the other teachers, who were impressed by his proactive attitude. The teachers had mentioned his positive approach and relationships with the pupils to the Headteacher who, at the end of the week, offered to write a reference for him if ever it were required. When John started his course, he was asked to complete an assignment on questioning. He consulted the notes he had made and, with some other research, he handed in a high-quality piece of work.

brilliant dos and don'ts

Do

✔ Do ask plenty of questions. The answers to any that come to mind might really help you in the first few weeks of your course.

✔ Do expect to stay behind after school one evening for the weekly meeting. The school may not ask you to do this, but if they haven't mentioned it, it would be wise to offer. It would

▶

give you a great insight into the important issues that need to be discussed. However, for the same reason, they may ask you not to attend because they may need to discuss confidential issues.

✔ Do speak to the class teachers in advance and ask if they would be happy for you to work with the pupils once the tasks have been set. This is polite, because they will have worked hard to plan that lesson, possibly without taking into account your presence. The fact that you have asked will make them think about how they can involve you, so you get the best experience possible.

✔ Do write *exactly* what a particularly inspiring teacher says. Upon further analysis, you may notice patterns in the way they speak and the directions they give that get the pupils to want to follow their instructions.

✔ Do allow the school to conduct a CRB check, if they ask. You will have to get used to this. You cannot work in a school without one, and many schools will require one just for the experience week. If you agree to it, they will take care of it.

Don't

✗ When writing to the school, don't say that the reason you are applying to that school is because it's the closest one to you. Show them that you have done some research.

 **brilliant** recap

The benefit you will receive from the experience weeks is entirely down to your own involvement. If you are proactive and make an effort to work with the teachers, you will learn much more about what it is to be a teacher. Be respectful of the fact that teachers and Headteachers are busy people, so don't expect them to drop everything to speak to you. However, if you offer to help in whatever way you can, they will be grateful and involve you in the lessons, so you will end the week feeling that it has been really useful. My recommendations are:

- Write well in advance of the time you are requesting the experience for.

- Speak to teachers in advance about ways in which you can be helpful.

- Tell them what kinds of things you will be looking for, based on the information you have received from the course provider, and ask if they mind if you make notes.

- Ask lots of questions in the staff room at lunchtime. My experience is that teachers quite enjoy talking about teaching!

CHAPTER 3

The course

There are a number of different types of teacher training course; go to Chapter 1 to compare them. However, the objectives and the way the courses achieve them are basically similar. So, whichever course you have chosen to do, I hope you find the advice in this chapter useful.

The whole reason you are doing this course is to become a good teacher. Guidance on the teaching itself is given in Part 3, but there are other things you will need to do, apart from the teaching, to be able to gain the Qualified Teacher Status (QTS). This chapter contains practical tips about working with teachers and fellow trainees, how to complete assignments and how to pass the compulsory QTS tests.

The people around you

I think it's really important to take advantage of having so many people around you.

My friend and I discussed recently how we both felt that we taught better this year than last. When I applied to become an Advanced Skills Teacher (AST), I must have been confident in my ability to teach. Yet, looking back on those lessons I delivered during the assessment, there are definitely things I would change. Perhaps that is why experienced teachers are happy to offer advice to trainee teachers. They have spent years learning and perhaps making mistakes that they wouldn't want you to have to make.

The teachers you are working with, the member of staff in school responsible for assisting and monitoring your progress (sometimes called the 'Professional Tutor', 'Professional Mentor' or 'Programme Manager') and the tutors at your training institution are all there to support you. They will have lots of experience, so will know what you are going through and can advise you on any issues to do with teaching or the pupils themselves.

I would also suggest that you should not be afraid to ask teachers if they have any resources you could borrow. During your course, you will spend hours making cards for pupils to match up or play other games with, presentations, information sheets and finding suitable Internet resources. However, if there are already some similar in existence, you can spend your time making something new. Teachers will really appreciate any contributions towards their resource collection. If you readily offer them your resources, it will remind them of things they have made and they will probably return the favour. I think it is also important that you ask teachers, if you feel it would be useful, what resources they think would work well with this particular lesson. They may tell you about a resource they've always wanted to make, but haven't had the time, and it might be an excellent idea.

 **brilliant** tip

To help you get to know some of the teachers, offer to help with one of the lunchtime or after-school clubs.

> if you have made something you found useful – offer it out

The other people that I really enjoyed working with were my fellow trainees. You will meet them during your training sessions, if not before. Again, these can be mutually beneficial relationships to build. If you have made something you found useful – offer it out. They will be grateful and will be likely to reciprocate. If you have had a good idea, share it. I still e-mail some people who were on my course to ask if they can think of exciting activities, when I am lacking inspiration.

brilliant tip

It is worth spending time making good resources – you may use them every year thereafter. Make sure you store them somewhere you will never forget, already categorised (for example, the year of the class and the subject you were teaching).

Of course, the thing that I found most valuable is the emotional support trainees give each other. I found quite often that when I started to tell a story that had been causing me some stress, other trainees helped me find the humour in it! If, when you are talking about a concern, you find that others have had similar experiences, it makes you feel less isolated. Of course, you may be able to offer each other valuable advice. In addition to all of this, if you are working with people who are in a similar situation to you, you may find that you are quite like-minded and it's always a good thing to be thrown together with people like that.

Completing assignments

You are very likely to be required to complete assignments to be able to pass your course (definitely if you are working towards a Masters). Whatever your assignments are, they will be designed really to get you thinking about teaching and learning processes. It will therefore be valuable to conduct formal interviews with pupils about how this issue affects them. Don't be worried about this; pupils love having their chance to speak. Consult the teachers in advance because it would be inappropriate and disorganised to ask during the lesson. They will help you to

<table>
<tr><td>

plan your questions in
advance

</td><td>

select pupils for the interview. Also
plan your questions in advance. If
it looks professional, the pupils will
take it even more seriously. To add

</td></tr>
</table>

to this, you will be able to include the questions as part of your
assignment.

---

brilliant tip

Involving pupils in your assignment will give you a better insight
than just reading the suggested literature. It will also make your
assignment different from everybody else's.

It is often useful to speak to other members of staff about their
experiences of the issue and also to quote them anonymously
in the assignment. Teaching is a job heavily dependent on your
ability to interact with others, so this is a good opportunity to
prove that you can do it. Your time with teachers will not need to
be on a formal interview basis, and could just be a quick chat in
the staff room, but let them know in advance what you're doing
and make notes so you don't forget what they have told you.
You may even consider finding out if there is a member of the
Senior Leadership Team who carries responsibility for the issue.
You could write to them in advance, giving them the title of the
assignment and letting them know how long you would like to
spend talking to them. With plenty of notice, they shouldn't have
a problem finding the time and may even be able to lend you
recent literature on the subject.

---

brilliant tip

When writing your assignments, refrain from using the names of
anybody you have spoken to, whether staff or pupils. Reassure them

in advance that this will be the case. The school might wish to receive a copy of your assignment and many people would like to be honest, without getting into trouble.

Of course, you will need to consult texts for your assignment. If you're not sure of how many references you should include, especially for the first assignment, ask your Mentor from the training institution to give you an idea of how many they feel would be appropriate. If you have been provided with a reading list, make sure you use it. Your trainers will have directed you to these documents to ensure you read the most up-to-date research.

brilliant tip

Ask your fellow trainees if they have come across some good literature for your assignments. Sharing these could save you all a lot of time.

brilliant example

Here are a couple of examples of possible assignments, with ideas of how you might tackle them creatively, in a way that involves working with students and teachers.

Discuss the differences in achievement between males and females in your subject or specialism

- Get some results from the teacher and do some statistical analysis (averages may suffice).
- Get some results from other subjects or specialisms (you may need to enlist the help of your Professional Tutor for this), to see if any differences you found in your chosen area are the same in others.   ▶

- Interview pupils of both genders to find out what they think.
    - Which kinds of activity do they enjoy?
    - Which activities do they dislike?
    - Do they see any differences in the way the two genders learn?
- Analyse the answers to see if it is the way the subject is taught that causes the differences.
- Ask teachers what they think about it.
- Consult some journal articles or books, using the library's referencing system.
- In your discussion, summarise your findings.
- Write a conclusion about how teaching could be improved to ensure neither gender is underperforming.

How can teachers encourage independent learning?

- Observe a sample of lessons, giving teachers plenty of notice and explaining the objectives of the observations. For each activity, rate it on how dependent the pupils were on the teacher for completing this task. Or, you might choose to take a percentage of how much of the lesson was spent on the students working independently. Write a discussion of your results.
- Set the pupils a task, with quite an open-ended question, such as 'explain the erosion of cliff faces', providing them with plenty of resources, and observe how they accomplish it. Write up your notes about this, which could be some descriptions of what the pupils did. If you notice anybody failing to work independently, speak to them about what they think they could do.
- Interview pupils, with questions such as:
    - Can you think of some tasks you've had to complete recently without the help of anybody?
    - Did you enjoy this? Why?
    - How much of your lesson do you think you should spend working like this?

- Do you think it helps you to learn more?
- Interview teachers, with questions such as:
  - What do you think is the value of independent learning?
  - What kinds of tasks might you set to encourage independent learning?
  - Approximately what proportion or percentage of your lessons is spent with the students working independently?
  - What do you think would help teachers to encourage independent learning? For example, are there any resources you think would be useful?
- Research from the available literature.
- Write a conclusion about what teachers can do to encourage independent learning.

brilliant tip

Invest in a Dictaphone, or use the one on your mobile phone or MP3 player to record the answers. That way, you could spend your time really listening to the answers, rather than frantically scribbling. Just check first that the people involved don't mind being recorded.

Passing QTS tests

As previously mentioned, to be able to pass the course, you must pass the QTS tests in Numeracy, Literacy and ICT. Some trainees dread them, but really, it is a very good thing that the government is checking that their teachers are up to a certain standard in these skills. Whatever your subject or specialism, these skills are in daily requirement and you will need to pass them on to your pupils. This is your chance to make sure you have got it right. They will be useful throughout your entire life.

For example, there is no way I would have been able to write a book without my QTS test in Literacy! My studying for it taught me a lot.

Because the end of the course can be quite stressful, with your final assessments, it is probably wise to take your QTS tests earlier in the course, rather than later. Also, if you do fail, it gives you plenty of time to book a retake. You can take the tests as many times as is necessary to pass them, at no extra cost to yourself. However, you have to book them for a certain venue at a certain time, which can be some hassle.

The tests are all less than an hour long. The numbers of questions are varied, but none of them require you to write paragraphs. They are all short answers, typed into a computer program, or a request for you to demonstrate a computer skill.

Sometimes, a school will allow you to take time off to do these tests, but the venues hold test sessions out of working hours, which could be more convenient and would prevent you from having to set cover work. You will be allowed a sheet of paper for making notes or calculations and further sheets are available upon request, which will need to be handed in at the end. You will find out at the end of the test whether or not you have passed.

there are practice tests available

There are practice tests available, with guidance (see the web address in Appendix 4). These are extremely useful. Another resource I found to be even more valuable is a range of books entitled 'Passing the ... skills test'. These books teach you all the skills you need to know and then give you practice questions. You can find the details of these books in Appendix 5.

brilliant dos and don'ts

Do

✔ Do share your experiences with other trainees. Also help each other out with ideas about the assignments.

✔ Do speak to teachers well in advance of the assignment's deadline. This means they will find time to help you and will be able to support you in speaking to their pupils, without having to change their own lesson plan.

✔ Do try to understand the value of the QTS tests. If we want the children of our society to have a good education, we must accept that the government needs to check teachers' spelling, grammar, mathematical ability and computer skills.

Don't

✘ Don't leave your assignments to the last minute. Extra research can take quite a lot of time, but it will make your assignment stand out from those written by people who referred to literature in the reading list only.

brilliant recap

Throughout your course, you will need to meet some other requirements, on top of your teaching load, to be able to achieve QTS. If you are struggling with this, it is acceptable to discuss it with your tutors, but you will still need to complete the assignments given and the QTS tests. They are there to make sure you are up to a certain educational standard and to make sure you have the ability to think deeply about issues in education. My recommendations are:

● Enlist the help of others, not only with your lessons, but with the assignments too.

- Involve the pupils and teachers when you write assignments, to be able to develop your own conclusions, rather than repeat what is in the literature.

- Be creative when completing your assignments.

- Complete your QTS tests as early as possible.

- Practise your QTS tests before taking the real ones, using the online tests and the available literature.

PART 2

Teaching
practice

CHAPTER 4

Entering your training school

Entering the school where you will be training to teach can be very daunting. It is highly likely that your first day will be a normal school day, not a training day, and as soon as you arrive you will notice that the teachers are rushing around because they will have a certain number of things they need to do before morning registration or first lesson. If you are in a large school, the teachers may not realise who you are or what you're doing there and may not stop to speak to you. There is one person, however, whose job it is to find you when you arrive. This is your Professional Tutor, although the title of the role may differ depending on the type of course you are doing (other examples include the 'Professional Mentor' and the 'Programme Manager').

Your Professional Tutor's job is to oversee your training within the school. They will have organised your timetable and spoken to the teachers with whom you will be working. They will have planned your in-school training sessions and they will expect you to be able to talk to them if ever you are having difficulties. They are also responsible for introducing you and showing you around.

The other member of staff you will be closely linked to is your Mentor in school. This is likely to be the teacher of the class that you will be working with in a primary school, or if you are in a secondary school, somebody in your Department; someone who will see you on a day-to-day basis. The Professional Tutor is usually a highly experienced member of staff, whereas the Mentor may have only been teaching for a few years and it can sometimes feel a bit easier to talk to them, knowing that the challenges you face will be fresh in their memory!

Your first day

Your first day is likely to involve a meeting between you, your Professional Tutor and any other trainee teachers that will be working there. You will be shown around the school and will find out where the staff room, toilets, assembly hall, sports hall (if different), library and classrooms are. You should be provided with a security pass for the school, which will probably be some kind of identity badge or card, so people who see you will know that you have permission to be there. If the Headteacher or Principal is around, you will hopefully have the chance to talk to them to discuss the school in terms of the catchment area, the grades the pupils have been achieving and the priorities of the school. You may even meet a group of pupils who either form the School Council, or who have been selected to speak to you about school life. Lunch may be provided (on this day only), for you to eat with other members of staff and possibly other trainees. You will also be taken to your classroom, if primary, or if secondary, shown around the Department in which you will be working. You will be introduced to the teachers, including your Mentor, and other staff, such as resource technicians.

During your first day, the information you should receive includes your timetable and your schedule of training sessions. You will probably get a login for the school network and even a map of the school if it's a big one! You should be given a calendar or diary for the school year, which will include the dates of after-school meetings, parents' evenings, mentoring days and open evenings, all of which you will be required to attend, if they take place on the days on which you are scheduled to be in school.

You should be told about what to do if you encounter any child protection issues, for example what you should say to the pupil and which member of staff you should report it to.

 **tip**

Things to take on your first day

- A diary for any meetings or events you are told about and to log any important information such as telephone numbers, usernames and passwords for the school network.
- A notebook and writing equipment.
- A laptop if you use one regularly.
- Lunch and a drink – just in case!

Establishing routines with teachers

If you are training to be a primary teacher, you will probably be working with just one class, although in larger schools the pupils are sometimes placed into sets, based on their ability, for Literacy and Numeracy. At these times, you will also encounter pupils from other classes. If you are working in a secondary school, your timetable will tell you which classes you will be working with and which teachers, plus the rooms in which those lessons take place. At first, you will be expected to attend your lessons as an observer. There is more information about how you can make these lesson observations most valuable in Chapter 5.

You will be introduced by the teacher in your first lesson. It may be worth discussing this with the teacher beforehand, to determine how they will do it. I always introduce trainee teachers as a teacher who will be working with us for a while, but I know of some people who have been introduced as trainee teachers. I don't see any problem with the pupils knowing that you are a trainee teacher because they know that everyone has to start teaching at some point. You can't blame some of them for wondering if that means that you'll be a pushover, but there are ways to stop that very quickly, discussed in Chapters 5 and 6. If you would prefer not to be introduced as a trainee teacher, or would just like to know what the teacher was planning to say, feel free to ask them before the lesson.

it is important to establish routines with teachers about communication

Not long after you start the course, you will be asked to take small parts of lessons, with the teacher present in the room. For this to work efficiently, it is important to establish routines with teachers about communication of lesson objectives, joint planning and the ordering of equipment and resources. Teachers very quickly get used to the fact that the only times they can communicate properly with each other are at break times, lunchtimes, after school (when they are looking forward to going home) or in their free periods (which they need for planning, preparation and assessment). If it feels that they can't find the time for you, try to understand this. It is always best if you agree times to talk in advance. If you give them options for various times, they are obliged to fit you into their busy schedule. After all, you cannot do well in your training year without it.

brilliant tip

Remember that your Professional Tutor and your Mentor are there to provide advice about any matters to do with the course, the school or your lessons if you would like it. You can also talk to them about any concerns you have about working with the teachers. There is also your Tutor in your training institution if you would prefer to talk to somebody outside the school.

When it comes to the time when you need to start lesson planning, it is important to find out your school's guidelines for how far in advance you provide the teachers with lesson plans, but you will also need to discuss it with the teachers themselves. The most organised members of staff will probably expect you to be just as efficient as they are. These may also be the kinds of teachers from whom you can learn the most. The class teacher will need to give you lesson objectives (what the pupils will need to have learned by the end of the lesson) and a few tips in advance. If applicable, they should also discuss with you the Health and Safety aspects of the lesson. Give them a copy of the lesson plan with enough time to allow them to look at it and get back to you with some suggested changes to activities or ideas. Then, you will need to make those adaptations. As a teacher who has worked with trainee teachers, I would expect the lesson plans two days in advance, or at the very minimum, 24 hours before the lesson. Even then, if you need to order different resources in response to the teacher's advice, then you may be relying on somebody else to prioritise that, or late nights for you!

It is important for you that the teachers with whom you are working are sympathetic, as it can be difficult to establish so many new routines, such as lesson planning in advance, ordering equipment, assessing work and preparing for meetings, all in addition to meeting deadlines with your training institution. However, it is crucial that you get into the habit of planning lessons in advance. If you enter a lesson without having contemplated the details of it, it could very quickly backfire, which could have severe implications for your relationships with your pupils.

The staff room

The staff room is quite an intimidating place. Many people will have been working in the school for many years and quite a few will have their own chair, in an unspoken kind of way. When you sit in it, you wonder why people give you a concerned glance. How you react to that is up to you, but it may be worthwhile to ask a friendly member of staff about it.

It is an unfortunate fact that some members of staff who are not working with you may see you as transitory, so may not invest the time or effort to speak to you. This makes it difficult to go into the staff room for the first time. But, there are always friendly people in there too, who will very quickly make you feel welcome by asking how you are getting on.

Relationships with other members of staff

Your experience of teaching will be enhanced if you form good relationships with staff, both in and outside your class or department. One good way of forming relationships quickly is to find out from your Mentor which teachers have particular skills in any aspect of teaching. Approach that teacher when they do not look as though they are in a rush, let them know that you have heard that they are considered to be highly skilled in … [whatever it is] and ask if you could observe them. Teachers are teachers by nature and they will enjoy educating you as much as they do the pupils. They will also be flattered!

teachers will enjoy educating you as much as they do the pupils

brilliant tip

Another good way to get to know staff is to help someone who runs a club. Make it one that you are interested in so you'll feel motivated to donate a lunch break every week to it. In fact, you will probably be required to do so for your course anyway and if you choose your club when you first get there, you will avoid having one dumped on you at a later date!

Other people you need to get on the right side of are the resource technicians. These are the people who do the photocopying, make any cards that you want, laminate them, or write letters home for you. If you are teaching practical lessons, such as Science, Technology or Art, they are also the people who make sure you get what you need for your lesson to run smoothly. The computer technicians are also incredibly useful to know. I have worked with some who have been good enough to come straight to my lesson if I have had technical difficulties. You need the support of these people and must not take them for granted. You may feel very rushed in school. It's not that you're any busier than other teachers, but you may not yet be used to the pace. Even so, it's really important to take the time to be polite and ask people how they are. I'm not saying that you should do it only because they help you sometimes. Of course, we all like to be considerate towards others anyway, but if resource technicians find you impolite, rude or arrogant, they may not prioritise your work!

Working with form tutors

If you are working in a secondary school, you will be assigned a form or tutor group to work with. Make sure you have met the tutor before the first session you are meant to attend. You can be assured that the Professional Tutor will deliberately have chosen a teacher for you to work with who is known for building positive relationships with their pupils. It is a great opportunity to see this person in action because they have very different duties in this role from those they have as a class teacher. A form tutor has an incredible impact on their pupils' behaviour and attitude in all of their lessons. It is wonderful to see how a teacher uses their knowledge of their pupils to help them achieve. If ever you wish to discipline a pupil in your attached form group, speak to the tutor first. They will know the pupils well and will be able to advise you of the best courses of action.

Encountering the pupils for the first time

find out what the
behaviour policy is

Before you go into your first lesson, find out what the behaviour policy is. This should be on the school website, so you may even be able to check it before you get to the school. For example, is there a traffic light system (amber means you need to watch your behaviour, red means the removal of certain privileges, 'time out' or detention and so on)? Is there a code (where 1 may mean a warning, 2 a detention or being moved to another part of the room, 3 a phone call home …)? Do not be afraid to use it right from the first moment you step into a classroom, or maybe even in the corridors before.

brilliant tip

If you are about to implement a reward or sanction in your first few weeks, check first with a teacher to make sure they feel it is appropriate. It may be that you are tempted to show the pupils who's boss immediately, but it is important to use a scaled series of sanctions, rather than jumping in at the most serious. A similar pattern may also be true when it comes to rewards.

Pupils are not stupid. They will know you're a trainee teacher and as I have already said, I don't think that's anything to be embarrassed about. However, you can be equally as important to them in both a positive way and a disciplinary way. You could still phone home to say that they had been working hard or alternatively that they hadn't completed their homework. The sooner you let them know that, the better. Be confidently encouraging to them as much as possible, and in a way that makes them realise that you know your opinion counts.

brilliant tip

Always ask your Mentor before phoning parents. Some schools have a policy of only allowing their permanent members of staff to do this.

brilliant dos and don'ts

Do

✔ Do arrive on your first day punctually and well equipped (see 'brilliant tip' on page 57). This is as much about ensuring that you do not get flustered as it is about creating a good impression.

✔ Do feel free to introduce yourself to anyone who appears to be wondering who you are.

✔ Do remember that it may take a few days or even a few weeks before you feel relaxed in this new environment.

✔ Do be authoritative around pupils from the outset.

✔ Do involve yourself in extra-curricular activities to help you get to know other members of staff.

Don't

✘ Don't be offended if a teacher doesn't seem to want to spend time answering your questions. It is likely to be because they are so busy themselves.

✘ Don't rely on casual chats at lunchtime to find out important information. Book meetings with people if necessary.

brilliant recap

Entering a training school can feel very intimidating, with lots of people rushing around, not seeming to notice you. But there are

▶

people in the school who have a role of helping you to excel in your time there. Because schools are such busy places, it is important to establish routines with people with whom you will be working closely to ensure you can both be efficient.

When you come to meet the pupils, act as a teacher from the outset. Remember you have the same rewards and sanctions available to you as any other teacher.

CHAPTER 5

Observing lessons

When you start your school experience, you will need to observe lessons being taught by qualified teachers. This is, as much as anything, a way of familiarising yourself with school life, which will probably be different from what you remember from your younger years. Lessons are structured differently now and ideas and technology have moved on enormously.

Of course, your main priorities when observing lessons include noticing what the teachers and pupils do and how they respond to each other. Plus, not all teachers are the same. They have different personalities, which will affect their relationships with their pupils. For this reason, you will not be expected to emulate them. But you will notice that all of the most effective teachers share some traits and habits. It is these that you can identify during your observation time.

It is very important to be just as professional when you are observing lessons as you would be teaching them. You must be there on time and behave appropriately throughout the lesson. Unbelievably, I have seen trainee teachers checking their mobile telephones for text messages while I was trying to teach the speed of light. If the pupils aren't allowed to do it, they will resent you for thinking that you are and they may perceive it to mean that you think you are above the rules. Pupils do not like that and neither will the teachers.

observing lessons is
an extremely tiring
experience

Observing lessons is an extremely tiring experience. You know that feeling of sitting down after a hard day, with the radio on, and that voice sending you to sleep? That's what it can be like in lessons sometimes. You may not be feeling particularly alert, because it might seem as though you are not required to do anything, but if you remain focused, you will be able to learn a lot from these people. I regularly ask other teachers if I can sit in on a lesson, because I think I can gain valuable skills and strategies from it. To a full-time teacher, the ability to observe others is a luxury and we all wish we could do it more, because everybody has their own particular strengths, and we all have our own weaknesses, or, more politically correct, areas for improvement.

Before the lesson

It is worth having a chat with the teacher before you observe their lesson, to set up some protocols. For example, when they are addressing the class as a whole group, where would they like you to sit? Are you happy to help them out if needed? For example, if they run out of paper, would you and to find some for them? When the pupils are working, is there a limit to how much help they would like you to give them? It would also be helpful for you to discuss how to handle it if a pupil asks you a question about the subject and you don't know the answer.

brilliant tip

It would be great if you could set up some regular communication, so you know what will be covered in the lessons that you will be observing. This will allow you to brush up in advance, and save the embarrassment of having to tell the pupil that you're not sure. You'll have to make sure you know it at some time anyway!

Here is a comprehensive list of things to look for during lesson
observations, in order to decide how you will teach and interact
with pupils:

Beginnings of lessons

- How do the pupils come into the room?
    - Do they line up outside?
    - Do they come straight in when they arrive?
    - Is there a school policy for this?
- What routines has the teacher established to get pupils to
  settle down?
    - Does the teacher have a small activity prepared, written
      on the board, or a worksheet on the desk?
    - Do pupils collect their own books, does the teacher give
      them out, or are they already on the desks waiting? Is
      there an established routine in which the students hand
      the books out?
    - Do they just keep chatting and walking around until
      they are given instructions by the teacher?
- Notice what the teacher does to:
    - Get the lesson started.
        - Do they shout until they have the pupils' attention?
        - Do they stand in silence at the front of the class?
        - Are the pupils in the habit of preparing themselves
          so the teacher has to do very little to get them
          settled?
    Get them to be quiet.
        - Shout out to get their pupils' attention?
        - Put their hand in the air, mirrored by the pupils, to
          form an agreed silence?
            - Any other visual gesture?

- Time the pupils and put the number of minutes on the board, which the pupils then realise will be deducted from their break time?
- Keep asking them to be quiet until they are?
- Are there any particular strategies they have? For example, I start to say calmly 'I'm waiting for ... Stephen, Shannon', which is usually followed by a quick apology from them.

Interaction between the teacher and the pupils

- What does the teacher do to:
  - Stop somebody from talking over them?
    - Challenge the pupil?
    - Make visual gestures (finger to the lips, hand in the air, or hand out in the direction of the pupil – discussed in Chapter 13)?
    - Shout?
    - Mark down on a piece of paper the names of the pupils who have spoken, the consequences of which are understood by the pupils?
  - Stop somebody from messing around?
    - Challenge the pupil?
    - Give a verbal warning?
    - Move the pupil?
    - Tactically ignore it?
- How does the teacher communicate generally during the lesson?
  - Do they establish silence before giving any instructions?
  - Do they write the instructions on the board?
  - Are the instructions written on cards or pieces of paper?

- Do they walk around and talk to all of the tables of pupils individually?
- Some teachers can communicate a lot without saying a word. Are there established visual cues to which the pupils respond?

● What tone of voice does the teacher adopt to speak to the pupils?
- Authoritative?
- Abrupt?
- Negotiating?
- As one would talk to a friend?
- Non-negotiable orders?
- Pleading?

● Do they always give reasons for their instructions?
- See Chapter 13 for more information on how to communicate in a way that makes pupils want to listen.

● How does the teacher praise pupils?
- What do they say?
  - Do the pupils respond to it well?
  - Are there lots of superlatives or are the comments based on observations or skills?
    - For example, do they say 'That was incredibly good, well done' or 'The way you mixed that paint gave you really clear lines, well done'?
- Is there a school system for logging any praise or achievement, such as merit points or stickers on a chart? Do the pupils respond well to these?
- Does the teacher tell pupils that they will be telephoning or writing home to congratulate them on their efforts?

Establishing routines

● How does the teacher:

    – Get pupils to move around the class sensibly?

        – Are there any habits that the teacher has already established?

        – Do they get the pupils to stand up and tuck their chairs in before they will allow them to continue?

        – Are there posters about the importance of safe behaviour?

        – Are there established areas where the pupils should or shouldn't go?

    – Get pupils to pack away?

        – Do the pupils choose to do it when they feel it is the end of the lesson?

        – Do they pack away of their own accord when the bell goes?

        – Does the teacher establish silence before they tell them to pack away?

        – Do they put their own books away or do they leave them on the desk?

        – If the teacher has lent equipment to pupils, do they ensure it is collected, or assume, based on habits and experience, that it will have been returned?

        – If the lesson involved practical elements, how is the equipment packed away?

            – Do the pupils do this?

            – Do the teacher and TA help?

            – If they have to wash things, is there an order for groups to go to the sink?

            – Does the teacher spread out the places for the equipment to be returned, in order to prevent everyone going to one area?

- Is there anything the teacher does to promote positive relationships between the pupils?

Teaching strategies

- What do you notice about the pace of the lesson?
  - Is it too fast, so that some pupils are struggling to meet all of the challenges?
  - Is it too slow, so that some pupils finish early, get bored and start to mess around?
  - Is it just right, so all pupils are able to learn and demonstrate their new skills and knowledge?
- Which activities do pupils seem to enjoy or gain the most understanding from?
- Which activities do not go so well? Do you have any thoughts about why this might be the case?
- How does the teacher work out who has performed well and who couldn't keep up with the pace?
  - Were there any activities that gave the teacher an on-the-spot idea of who understands what (see Chapter 8)?
  - Will they learn later from book marking?
- How does the teacher ensure all of the pupils' individual needs are met?
  - Is there a TA, and if so, are they well directed?
    - How does the teacher do this?
  - Are there any special resources provided for pupils with specific learning needs, including those who learn much faster and easier than others?
  - Are there any pupils in the room who have not found any parts of the lesson accessible? What would you do differently?

> ☼ **brilliant** tip
>
> You will probably need to make some notes during observations, whether for an assignment or just for your own use. Understand that the teacher will naturally be very intrigued to know what you are writing and may be tempted to glance at them as they walk past! Also, sneaky pupils may try to take a look when you are not watching.

you will witness many different strategies

You'll notice that all of the above points contain different possibilities. The beauty of observation is that you will witness many different strategies, from which you will find some that you choose to use. Or, you may decide to adapt some, or make up your own entirely, which again is fine, and easier to do when you've seen some others in action.

> ☼ **brilliant** tip
>
> Be prepared for the teacher to ask you at the end of the lesson what you thought went well and what you thought could have gone better. One tactful way of addressing this latter question is to discuss the pupils' responses, rather than the teacher's actions.

After the lesson

At the end of the lesson, there may be some time for you to discuss what you observed. Feel free to ask any questions about what you noticed and why the teacher did it (so long as it is not in a disapproving way). There will be many times when you will feel that a certain situation would have been best tackled in a different way. It is great that you are thinking analytically like this, but you would be wise to think hard about how to approach it in discussion with the teacher, if that's what you plan to do. Teachers may do things that you don't think are such a good idea based on their experiences of past lessons and the pupils themselves, so it is very important to be tactful and open-minded when talking about what you saw. Also, you don't want to offend someone who will be imparting useful knowledge to you!

> be tactful and open-minded when talking about what you saw

You will have seen some things that you thought worked really well, whether they were activities or ways in which the teacher interacted with the pupils. It would be good for helping to build your relationship with the teacher if you talk to them about it. You may wish to ask in what situations this strategy is appropriate, or what gave them the inspiration to do it.

brilliant dos and don'ts

Do

✔ Do be empathetic with the teachers. Some people feel vulnerable being observed and will worry about how you will judge them. Remember that lessons do not always go to plan, but you may still be able to pick up great tips about how teachers can deal with unforeseen circumstances.

✔ Do be professional. For example, don't keep on chatting to the pupils while the teacher is trying to attract the whole class's attention.

✔ Do aim to learn some subject knowledge from these lessons. Also, remember to make notes on the activities the teacher used to teach it.

▶

✔ Do ask if you can make copies of any resources you find to be particularly effective. It'll save you hours and if you offer to do the copying, they can't really refuse!

Don't

✘ Don't see observation as a waste of time. You will, if vigilant, learn a lot from it.

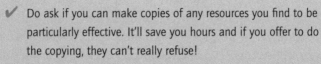 **brilliant** recap

Remember to stay on the ball when you are observing lessons. There is much to learn from them. Make notes about things that worked and things that didn't go so well: routines that have been established, methods of communication, how to maintain positive relationships, the engagement of pupils in the activities and the ways in which pupils are assessed. Always bear in mind though, that the teacher may not be able to resist glancing over your shoulder to see what you have written.

You may have a discussion with the teacher after the lesson. Tell them about the things that impressed you or that you noticed the pupils responded well to. Be tactful when talking about the things that you don't think you would use yourself.

CHAPTER 6

Preparing for your first lessons

At a time deemed to be appropriate, the class teacher will ask you to start teaching the lessons. They will ask you either to take a small section of the lesson, or to team teach with them, or, unlikely to begin with, teach a whole lesson.

The first thing you need to know is what the pupils are expected to have learned by the end of the session, known as the 'objectives'. You will then need to familiarise yourself with this topic at their level. You could do this by looking at the textbooks available to them. Next, of course, you will need to learn it to a higher level, to prepare yourself for any questions you might be asked. It's not necessarily a bad thing to be unable to answer a question and there are certainly some good ways to handle it. I find that if I say something like 'What a good point – I hadn't thought of that. I'll do some research and get back to you next lesson', most pupils are satisfied and the person may feel justifiably proud that they had considered something the teacher hadn't. I have known colleagues who will return the question with 'Good question – you can all find out for homework!' I worry that this will put pupils off asking questions in the first place – an activity that should actually be encouraged. But, regardless of all that, pupils will start to feel safe in your hands if you are able to answer their questions confidently.

 **tip**

Ask the teachers if you can borrow a copy of each of the textbooks that you may be required to use. This will help you plan lessons when you are at home.

It is not lazy or unskilled to ask the teacher how they would usually teach this topic. They may have some excellent tried and tested ideas. If you think they are good, feel free to use them. If you can think of other ideas, the teacher really shouldn't be offended if you would like to try something different. With whatever you do have in mind, you have to ask yourself – would you enjoy these activities? Would you and your peers have done so when you were younger? Be really honest with yourself, because if you set an activity that the pupils find boring or that they cannot understand, you may suffer during the lesson because either of those outcomes can lead to challenging behaviour.

Find out what the pupils will have learned during the previous lessons. Of course, you may have been present for these. It is important to know this so that you can talk about it when you are teaching and take it into account when you are planning. You may even need to recap it at the beginning of your lesson.

Objectives

The second question you must address is whether or not the activities you have planned will lead to the pupils meeting the objectives of the lesson. Even if the pupils are fully engaged with the work and seem to be learning a lot, the lesson could be considered to be unsuccessful if what they have learned is unrelated or only slightly related to the lesson objectives. One formally recognised aspect of a successful lesson is that the vast majority or all of the pupils fully meet the lesson objectives, which were originally prescribed by the government as part of the curriculum and that we are obliged to deliver.

Special Educational Needs

You must consider the individual pupils that will need particular thought during your planning. These include pupils with Special Educational Needs (SEN – see Chapter 9), such as:

- those who learn at a slower rate than others;
- those with literacy or numeracy difficulties;
- those who learn at a faster rate than others and more deeply;
- those who have social, emotional or behavioural difficulties;
- those who have specific physical needs.

The class teacher will know who these pupils are and should have access to their Individual Education Plans (IEPs). These are documents highlighting the pupils' difficulties and how the teacher should address them. It is important to familiarise yourself with these because you might need to think about preparing slightly different resources or activities for these pupils. Or, you will certainly need to bear it in mind when planning the questions that you will ask them as part of class discussions. You may also need to think about which pupils they would benefit most from working with. Consult Chapter 9 for more ideas.

For those with social, emotional or behavioural issues, you will need to know if there are any pupils who they should be kept apart from. Are there certain ways of talking to them? You may need to ensure they receive lots of praise when they do something well or if they settle down as soon as they come into the lesson. They may have certain areas of focus that you will need to be aware of.

Learning styles

Your school will hopefully have assessed the pupils' preferred learning styles – visual, auditory or kinaesthetic (see Chapter 7). If you can find out what each pupil's preferred style is, you will know which kinds of activities would be most effective in your lessons. Chapter 7 provides ideas of such activities.

brilliant tip

Get a copy of the seating plan in advance of the lesson. This shows who is sitting where. If you have it in front of you while you are teaching, you can use names to ask pupils questions, provide instructions or correct behaviour, which is far more effective than saying 'You, second in from the left'.

Rewards and sanctions

make sure you know the school's behaviour policy

Before your first lesson, make sure you know the school's behaviour policy. The pupils will start to see you as somebody with influence if you are able to talk about the school's systems, using the correct terminology. Find out the method of recording misdemeanours and what these records are called (for example 'action points' or 'concern notes'). Once you start to mention these, the pupils will know that you mean business! Conversely, a similar feeling will occur if you talk about the school's praise system. Make sure you know how to acknowledge good performance and behaviour and try to do this at least once in your first lesson, to let them know that you will be looking for positive things and would like to focus on achievement.

brilliant tip

You may have noticed some pupils who you think might cause you some difficulty. Ask the teacher how they deal with these pupils. They may have some good tips on how to get them to work well with you.

Health and Safety

Consider it a priority to ensure that you have met any Health and Safety requirements. It is unlikely that a teacher will give you any kind of practical task to teach for your first

> ensure that you have met any Health and Safety requirements

lesson, but you might need to tackle this aspect before long. If so, you must make sure you know if you are using any substances or equipment that is dangerous to the pupils and what you and the pupils need to do to eliminate or justifiably reduce the risk. It might be something simple. For example, if you are using wallpaper paste for papier-mâché, you will need to make sure it doesn't go near their mouths and gets washed off their hands afterwards, or if you are walking in the school field looking for something, ensure that the pupils do not leave the school grounds. If your lesson involves chemicals or certain types of equipment, such as those used in Technology, you will need to read the risk assessment that the school has already written, or maybe if you are trying something new, write one yourself, with the teacher's help.

Lesson planning

So, now you have the objectives and ideas of how you will allow your class to meet them. It is important to give the lesson plan to the teacher with lots of notice, preferably at least two days. You

give the lesson plan to the teacher with lots of notice

will need to have included the lesson objectives, the activities you plan to use, plus the details of any provision that you have decided upon for those pupils with SEN. If appropriate, you will also need to include any resources you require from other members of staff and give them this list as soon as possible. There is more information about how to write a good lesson plan in Chapter 11.

Other things you will need to think about and may even find useful to write in your lesson plan are the kinds of things you will say. It sounds, and is, laborious, but I did it for my first few lessons and it really helped to prevent me from feeling flustered. It will encourage you to think about what you will do or say to get the lesson started and what you will do or say if a pupil starts to talk over you. If you need the pupils to get up to move around or collect something, remind yourself of what you will do or say to make sure they do it sensibly. Think really carefully about all of the instructions you will give. There are many things that you may assume the pupils will or won't do, but that they actually won't think about. Giving them clear instructions, even if they are simple reminders, will really help, and won't have to sound patronising.

Thinking these things through in advance will not only enable you to be organised, but will also send a message to the pupils that you know what you are doing. For example, it may seem straightforward to say to the pupils 'Come and collect the worksheets', but if you pick certain people per table to collect them for the group, it will prevent people crowding around, which can lead to some disruption. If you want to demonstrate something, it will be useful to have decided beforehand where you would like people to sit, to be able to see it. Otherwise, they will move around themselves and discreetly end up sitting next to their friends, and might be tempted to chat with them.

When you are teaching your first lessons, you will have lots of different things to think about: pupils' names, their behaviour, your subject knowledge, the resources you have prepared and their order. It is reassuring to have prepared as much of this prior to the lesson as possible. For example, if you use PowerPoint (or similar presentation program) to take the pupils through the lesson, it will also take you through it. On that presentation, you will include the objectives, links to websites or other files, pictures, questions that you have planned to ask, and their answers! This gives you much less to have to think about off the top of your head and gives you a chance to think about other things that might not come naturally, such as behaviour management (see Chapter 13).

Your position as a trainee teacher

Pupils will build respect for you, as they will any member of staff, if you are well organised, know your subject knowledge (which might involve revising it a few days before), plan inspiring lessons and value their education. The fact that you are a trainee teacher will then have no bearing on their attitude towards you.

In the first few weeks of your teaching, the teacher will always be expecting to step in at some point, not because you're incompetent, but because they cannot expect you to be experienced right from the beginning. You will encounter many situations that you had not predicted, and you may not know how to handle them instantly. Teachers know that and they also know that it will come with experience, which is what you are trying to gain. If they interrupt your lesson, they should do it in a subtle way, pretending for instance that they need to talk to you about something. If they do that, don't be embarrassed. Take their feedback with grace. In addition, if ever you feel that you need their help or advice during a lesson, don't be scared to ask for it. To see their teacher and you working together to make sure you deliver the lesson well sends a positive message to the pupils. Towards the end of the year, you should be taking lots of whole lessons with very little input from the teacher. But at any point, if you are asking for their advice in order to make your lessons more effective, they cannot criticise you for it.

Finally ...

In the classroom, don't be afraid to use your own style. You don't have to mimic the teachers you are working with. Good teachers will enjoy seeing other teaching styles and are likely to learn from you. They will often want to use any resources that you make and it is important to give them a copy every time.

brilliant dos and don'ts

Do

- ✔ Do think through your lesson or section of lesson step by step.
- ✔ Do consider what might go wrong and think of solutions in advance.
- ✔ Do ask the teacher for tips on working with this class or teaching this topic.
- ✔ Do approach the lesson in a different way from the suggestions of the teacher if you feel it would be appropriate. Still run it by the teacher though, in case there are any reasons for not doing it your way.
- ✔ Do give the teacher a copy of any resources you make.
- ✔ Do prioritise establishing your relationship with the class over the lesson content in the first lesson. However, being organised is very good for that relationship!

Don't

- ✗ Don't enter your first lesson expecting the pupils to be a nightmare. They will pick up on this and will respect you more if you look for positive things to highlight.

✗ Don't panic if the lesson doesn't go to plan. This happens to even the most experienced teachers and the class teacher will be able to catch up on any missed work.

 **brilliant** recap

Your first few lessons can be very daunting. You may worry about the topic, the activities, the judgement of the teacher and the pupils' behaviour. The more you think about the practical aspects, the better prepared you will be. The teachers will be looking for things that go well and areas for development, because they are required to do so. They will also bear in mind that you are not yet a qualified teacher and will be lacking in some skills needed for the job. Otherwise, why would you need to train?

Your style will develop over time and you may not know at the outset what you want it to be. That is perfectly acceptable. The necessary things are meeting the objectives of the lesson, making your activities accessible to those with SEN, meeting the Health and Safety requirements and building positive relationships with the pupils. Your techniques and strategies will improve over time, and, to speed up that progress, don't hesitate to ask for advice, even if it means finding a time when you can do it discreetly during the lesson.

PART 3

Ideas for delivering high-quality lessons

CHAPTER 7

Learning styles

I f you were standing at a door with a keypad, trying to remember the code, how would you do it? Would you find yourself trying to picture the code written down? Would you be able to recall hearing the code? Would you try typing it in, hoping that the process will help you to remember which keys you pressed and in which order? Your answer to this will help you to work out your preferred learning style: whether you are predominantly a visual, auditory or kinaesthetic learner (V, A or K).

VAK learning

Our brains are anatomically very similar, but we all use the different parts of our brain to varying degrees. There are a number of proposed reasons for this, genetics being one

> we all use the different parts of our brain to varying degrees

and environmental influence (what kinds of things we grew up doing) being another, but regardless, we have to consider our pupils' differences when we are planning and teaching our lessons.

Whether our pupils are visual, auditory or kinaesthetic learners depends on which parts of their brain they rely on most when learning. We must not categorise people as solely visual learners, auditory learners or kinaesthetic learners, however, because everybody is different and some pupils may rely equally on all three learning styles. To add to that, there are a few other learning styles, including digital (like 'Rain Man', where things are processed as data), olfactory (smell) and gustatory (taste), but we are not required to consider these in our planning, as they could make it quite difficult! However, if you are training to teach Food Technology, you may notice that some pupils are particularly influenced by smell and taste. Maybe the best chefs are olfactory and gustatory learners. There are also other ways of learning that inspire people, such as musical, naturalistic and linguistic. Good teachers will introduce a variety of activities so these are covered at some point.

Whether somebody is predominantly a visual, auditory or kinaesthetic learner may be apparent from a young age. There are links in Appendix 4 to find out what your and your pupils' preferred learning styles are, but here follows a guide. You will notice that many of the statements are generalisations and you might feel that not all statements apply to you and the pupils you are working with. That is because everybody uses other learning styles to some extent.

Visual learners

Visual learners are particularly stimulated by things they see. These pupils may like to see animations when you are trying to explain a theory. They may find it better to draw posters containing annotated diagrams than to write a large passage.

Sometimes, it can be easy to detect a visual learner by listening to the pupil's language:

- 'It looks like ...'
- 'I see what you mean.'
- 'I can't see how that could work.'
- 'It appears to me that ...'

In fact, you may also be able to deduce from a visual learner's eye movements which parts of the brain they are using. When we are concentrating, our eyes tend to move towards the area of the brain that we are drawing the information from. If, after you have asked a question, the pupil looks diagonally up, either to the left or the right, they are likely to be visualising a picture to be able to help them answer.

Tips for working with visual learners

Visual learners can learn things simultaneously. They can see one diagram or animation and get lots of information from it in a short amount of time. They respond well to a fast pace of talking and a high tone of voice. Most people are predominantly visual learners.

Auditory learners

Auditory learners will learn from hearing things. These pupils will learn from hearing what you say. Auditory learners may find it useful to be able to record long passages into a Dictaphone, in order to play it back later. Pupils that learn mostly by listening will make up only 30 per cent of everybody you teach, which is evidence that you should not teach mostly by talking at your pupils.

Again, language can give us clues that people are auditory learners. For example:

- 'I hear what you're saying.'
- 'I'll call on you later.'
- 'That rings a bell.'

When auditory learners are trying to recall something, they may look directly to the left or to the right.

Tips for working with auditory learners

Auditory learners learn things sequentially. They prefer to understand the first step before they move on to the next step. They prefer a slower pace to visual learners, with a varied tone of voice. Auditory learners may be talkative, which might require certain control measures from you, like not sitting them next to other auditory learners so they don't keep chatting while you are trying to talk to the class. Auditory learners may read quite slowly.

Kinaesthetic learners

These pupils will learn well by doing something. They may be the people who excel in practical subjects such as Science, Technology and PE. It's true for everybody that doing something creates neural pathways in the brain, which makes it easier to do it the next time, but these pupils are particularly reliant upon learning in that way.

The kinds of things that kinaesthetic learners may say include references to feelings or sensations, such as:

- 'I'm not really feeling it.'
- 'Get to grips with ...'
- 'Pain in the neck!'

When trying to remember something, kinaesthetic learners are likely to look to the bottom right (or bottom left if they are left-handed). This is towards the location of the kinaesthetic processing part of the brain.

Tips for working with kinaesthetic learners

Predominantly kinaesthetic learners make up the smallest proportion of the three learning styles. They prefer the pace of conversation to be slow. They also find it difficult to sit for long periods of time and they may be fidgeters! Some would therefore find it of benefit to be allowed to doodle during lessons. I know how contentious this is and some might see doodling as an activity of boredom or distraction. However, research by the University of Plymouth (Andrade 2010) has shown that some people remember things that they hear better if they were doodling when they were listening to it.

brilliant tip

If you do want to allow your pupils to doodle, check with the class teacher first. They may have been encouraging the pupils not to do it.

For effective learning to take place in your lessons and for all of the pupils to find your lessons enjoyable and worthwhile, you need to be catering for the needs of all three different learning styles. Give every one of your pupils something to remember!

brilliant tip

Ask the class teacher or your Professional Tutor if the school has conducted learning style tests on the pupils in your placement school. If not, seek permission to take your class into a computer suite to test themselves on the following website:

http://www.brainboxx.co.uk/A3_ASPECTS/pages/VAK_quest.htm

Of course, there are others. You just have to type 'online VAK test' into a search engine. If your school hasn't got the profiles yet, they will be really impressed when you suggest it!

Activities for the V, A and K learning styles

Below are some examples of the types of task each style of learner will find useful for them to be able to learn.

Visual

- Animations
- Videos
- Pictures
- Posters
- Drawings
- Cartoons
- Games
- Telling a story through mime or freeze framing
- Making photo stories to be projected on the board
- Dance
- Photographs
- Maps
- Graphs
- Slide shows
- Simulations
- Using different colours to show different parts of words.

Auditory

- Writing a story to be read out
- Asking questions to the group
- Discussions
- Music
- Radio interview
- News bulletin to be performed
- Narrated role play
- Reading aloud
- Debates.

Kinaesthetic

- Role plays
- Making board games for others to play
- Practical activities, such as experiments or practising techniques
- Making models of something you have just taught using a variety of materials, e.g. Plasticine
- Acting out a concept you have just taught, e.g. particles
- Collecting relevant things from around the school
- Matching cards
- Using rhythm to remember phrases or orders of things
- Creating mind maps
- Interactive whiteboard activities (see Chapter 10)
- Giving presentations
- Simulations
- Writing mathematical symbols in the air with their fingers.

brilliant tip

Try grouping your pupils so they are sometimes working with people of a similar learning style and set them a challenge related to that learning style. At other times, try grouping them with people of different learning styles, asking them to present their work in visual, auditory and kinaesthetic ways. This helps them to understand the relevance of their preferred style to their own learning.

Using your awareness of your pupils' learning needs to give instructions

Your awareness of VAK learning is important when giving instructions. Remembering that there will be people in your

awareness of VAK
learning is important
when giving instructions

class, all with slightly different learning styles, will encourage you to think about the things you could do to help them access what you are trying to teach:

- Repeat the same statement in different ways.
  - There is some truth in the fact that we see what we want to see, hear what we want to hear and even feel what we want to feel. If we repeat phrases in different ways, addressing the different learning styles, it will help to omit any inaccuracies that pupils have seen, heard or felt. For example, when giving an instruction, try saying it, demonstrating it and even getting pupils to practise doing that thing in front of you. The latter does not apply just for practical subjects. It also works for teaching habits, such as tucking chairs under tables quietly or moving around the classroom sensibly.
  - As well as repeating instructions, it may even be beneficial for you to write them on the board, if they are particularly important, for the visual learners. Conversely, auditory learners tend not to respond well to written instructions, so if you are giving out a worksheet, you may have to hold it up in front of the class before they start, to tell them the instructions, even if they are written on the sheet.

brilliant tip

Don't be afraid to set pupils tasks that are not in accordance with their learning style. Make sure they know that they will be a better learner if they try to adapt to other learning styles sometimes. In fact, the more we use an area of our brain, the more our body will make neurones for that area, so it is worth practising with all the learning styles.

Using your knowledge of learning styles for effective communication

You can also use this theory to help you communicate effectively. I'm sure you've heard the old adage that a very small percentage of our learning comes from what people say, a huge percentage comes from visual gestures, including facial expressions, and information is also received by the tone of voice. Visual learners respond particularly well to facial expressions. I often feel a bit like a drama queen when I exaggerate my facial expressions, but it's for the visual learners, especially the ones at the back of the room. I do wonder if it will give me wrinkles at a faster rate though! Auditory learners respond well to changes in the tone of voice, which might be why there are common stereotypes about some less effective teachers speaking in monotone. Kinaesthetic learners will want to touch and feel things, so if ever you can use the opportunity to pass things around the class and let the pupils explore them, go for it.

As discussed in Chapter 14, we can use our knowledge of VAK learning to influence people. For example, if you are having trouble motivating somebody, you could get them to

we can use our knowledge of VAK learning to influence people

imagine results day. To a visual learner, try asking 'What can you see happening on results day?' To an auditory learner, ask 'What do you think people will say to you if you get a level 5?' To a kinaesthetic learner, ask 'How are you going to feel if you get an A*?' This will help make them realise that these things could actually happen. Your influence could be increased by using the language of their learning style (see above) and adapting the speed and tone of your voice to that of theirs. It will help to create a feeling that you are on the same wavelength.

brilliant tip

It certainly doesn't hurt to communicate with your pupils about their learning styles, especially if you are working with older pupils, about to sit GCSEs or A-levels. It could really help them to plan their revision activities.

One other thing worth noting is that pupils' learning is also affected by their experiences in life, and not just those in your subject. There may be a reason for them not understanding an aspect of what you are trying to teach, whether it is to do with their learning style or things they have done in the past. The brain works strangely and unpredictably sometimes. Try not to lose patience with them!

brilliant dos and don'ts

Do

- ✔ Do try to speak to people when they appear to be distressed in a similar speed and tone of voice as theirs. However, if they are shouting, you don't have to shout back.
- ✔ Do have a checklist on every lesson plan where you can tick off V, A and K. This will make sure that you have accounted for all three of the learning styles.

Don't

- ✘ Don't be too hard on yourself about matching learning styles when communicating. It's most important if they are worried or upset, to help put your pupils at ease. However, it's equally as valuable to just be yourself at other times because they would much prefer a relaxed teacher to one that seems to be distracted by such issues.
- ✘ Don't allow pupils to feel that if the task is not directed towards their learning style, they don't have to do it. Remind them that life isn't like that in the workplace and they could use the opportunity to train their brain.

 **brilliant** recap

An understanding of the way our pupils learn can allow us to plan the most effective lessons. Your pupils may be predominantly visual, auditory or kinaesthetic learners, or a mixture of two or all three of them. We need to include in each of our lesson plans activities that cater to all of our pupils' needs. This means including at least one activity well suited to visual learners, one good for auditory learners and one for kinaesthetic learners. We can also use our understanding of VAK learning to improve communication with our pupils and even to have more influence over them, by adapting our language, speed of speech and tone of voice. Consult Appendix 5 for more information.

CHAPTER 8

Assessment for learning

This chapter is about making sure that all of your and your pupils' efforts are worthwhile. It is imperative that during every lesson you are able to analyse the progress of your pupils; who has learned what you wanted them to have learned from that lesson, who has struggled and who has excelled themselves? This is because those who are having some difficulty in understanding will need some extra help, either there and then, or by way of activities planned for subsequent lessons. Your intervention could involve an alternative way of explaining the material, or it could factor in the use of a Teaching Assistant (TA) to work with them on an individual or smaller-group basis (see Chapter 9). Those who appear to be exceeding your expected level of progress will also need further guidance. They could be 'Gifted and Talented' and it is our responsibility to ensure that we provide them with the ability to make exceptional progress in our lessons. To add to that, failure to stimulate the brains of these pupils can lead to them becoming bored and then disruptive. A significant proportion of bad behaviour in schools is exhibited by very intelligent pupils who may feel that their time is being wasted in lessons, because they are covering things that they either knew already, or understood within the first five minutes of arriving.

There are many ways in which we formally assess learning, in order to report the levels or grades. This type of end of topic/year/Key Stage assessment is called assessment *of* learning, otherwise known as summative assessment. However, something that is thought to lead to more effective education is assessment *for* learning (AfL), or formative assessment. This involves pupils being assessed, but then being given the chance to improve based on the feedback they are given.

There is a growing understanding that exams are not necessarily an accurate way of assessing pupils' abilities and that we can gauge a pupil's progress in many ways, such as what they can make, do, say, write or present. Their progress is also helped by the allowance of time to think and create; to show you what they know in their own way.

Levels and grades

Before we move on, I think it's important to establish the grading systems. National Curriculum levels range from 1 to 8, where level 1 is what pupils would be expected to achieve during the first couple of school years and level 8 is exceptional perform- ance at the end of year 9 (approximately 14 years of age). They are also subdivided into C, B and A. The A sublevel is higher than the C sublevel, so somebody working at a level 5A is two sublevels above somebody who is working at a level 5C. Some people (teachers and pupils included) have found this system confusing, so some schools have started to use an alternative of H (Higher), M (Middle) and L (Lower) for the sublevels. For example, a 5H pupil is two sublevels higher than a 5L pupil.

For your information, the government expect pupils to move up at least two sublevels a year, for example from a 2A to a 3B. We also have expectations of our pupils which we share with them in the form of a target grade. However, it would be inaccurate for us just to add two sublevels on to their original grade to form their target grade. This is why it is important to be able to assess accurately throughout the whole year to see if the pupil's target grade needs to be changed. It is not satisfactory to keep it as it is if they have already met it consistently within the first few weeks of the year.

In Key Stage 4, there are various grading systems. For example, there's the GCSE that is graded at A*–G and the BTEC and Diploma are becoming more popular, which are graded at a Pass, Merit or Distinction. As a very generalised rule (I say that because every individual is different and it is unacceptable for us to fall back on this instead of assessing accurately), a pupil achieving a level 5 at the end of Key Stage 3 will be expected to achieve a 'C' grade at GCSE. A pupil at a level 6 will be expected to achieve a 'B' and one at a level 7, an 'A' or an 'A*'.

Target grades

A pupil's target grade is the grade that they should have achieved by the end of the year or Key Stage. This will be formulated from a number of factors, including results from Cognitive Ability Tests (CATs, which are not statutory and only some schools use), National Curriculum Assessment (NCA) results or other previous teacher assessments. Of course, if your pupils are in their first year of school education, you will have very little information to go on.

It is important to introduce regular discussion about target grades with our pupils because it is good for them to have something to compare their attainment to. For pupils to

> introduce regular discussion about target grades with pupils

feel safe in this discussion, we must establish an environment in which progress compared to target grades, rather than the specific grade itself, is celebrated. You could even provide pupils with an individual progress chart that you will colour code, so that the grades are highlighted in green for 'above target', orange for 'on target' and red for 'below target'. Therefore, somebody who achieves two levels below another pupil could still have their grade coloured in green, which shows success. It is important to ensure that when you are talking to somebody who is working below target, you use positive language, expecting success in the future, such as 'So if we work on … together, it will be improved next time'.

brilliant tip

Before you discuss pupils' grades with them, check with the class teacher to see if they already have systems for doing this. Also, check that they agree with your levels.

In-class assessment

Assessing Pupils' Progress (APP)

There is now a movement towards sharing performance criteria, known as level descriptions (see page 114), with the pupils and allowing them numerous chances to work towards higher levels. This new method of formal assessment is known as Assessing Pupils' Progress (APP) and allows you to record levels based on what you have observed during the lesson or the work that pupils have produced, even after suggestions for improvement.

APP is expected to be used for the core subjects at Key Stages 1, 2 and 3 and for ICT at Key Stage 3. For more information on APP, go to the link in Appendix 4. However, APP is not the only form of AfL that you can use in the classroom and many AfL techniques can also be used in Early Years and Key Stage 4.

Further assessment by the teacher

not all assessment has to be formal

Not all assessment has to be formal. You will always need an idea of how your pupils are progressing, even if you do not intend to record it. There are ways of assessing the performance of all of your pupils within the lesson and it might sometimes make you realise that actually the message hasn't got through at all. If you realise that the pupils haven't understood what you have been teaching, you might need to stop and adjust the rest of your lesson accordingly.

The kinds of activities that can be used for this type of assessment include:

- thumbs up/thumbs down for true/false;
- answers or diagrams on miniature white boards;
- holding up cards in the correct order;
- having sections of the room labelled 'A, B, C, D' and getting pupils to move to the area of the room corresponding to the correct answer to a multiple choice question (or more recently, sending their answers through a Virtual Learning Environment voting system – see Chapter 10);
- levelled quizzes – so pupils choose which level of question to answer, but get more points for answering higher-level questions;
- getting pupils to act out concepts/personalities;
- play your cards right (or temperatures right or sizes right or distances right ...) so they have to shout out 'higher' or 'lower';
- making models of something you have just taught about, e.g. with Plasticine;
- watching presentations by pupils of research or a skill that has been learned, for example a Drama technique or the ability to use a certain piece of equipment.

All of these activities allow you to observe what learning has taken place and ensure that you will not need to wait until the next book-marking session in order to assess progress.

> ☀ **brilliant** tip
>
> Be inventive. AfL methods can be taken from popular quiz shows,
> such as 'Who wants to be a Millionaire?' – anything current to grab
> their attention.

Questioning

It is brilliant to have those pupils in our lessons who are able
to, and want to, answer all of the questions. But what are the
other pupils doing at the time? How much do they know? What
have they learned? The really keen pupils are very distracting
and it is always tempting to take their answers. But, we really
shouldn't allow these habits to develop because under these
circumstances, it is easy for the other pupils to switch off. More
effective would be to establish a 'No hands up' rule.

> ☀ **brilliant** tip
>
> A good way of encouraging the 'No hands up' rule is to use a
> randon name picker, such as the one available on http://classtools.
> net, which takes the form of a fruit machine.

It is best to try to ask a question to each pupil every lesson, either
as part of a discussion or when they are completing the tasks.
It is also more effective if you alter the level of your questions
depending on the pupil's ability. For example, for somebody
working at a lower level, you could ask a question that involves
a short, straightforward recall answer, such as 'What can you tell
me about the snake that allows it to merge in with its habitat?'
A higher-level question than this would be one that tests understanding, such as 'Why is the snake that colour?' Above that
would be one that encourages the pupil to apply their knowledge
to a new situation, such as 'Now we know about the snake, can

you tell me how the lion is adapted to its environment?' Higher pupils would then be able to analyse information, such as data on animals' habitats in relation to their colouring. Above that would be the ability to design or synthesise something themselves, based on this knowledge. For example, you could give them information about a habitat and then get them to describe a new animal that could live there. See Marzano and Kendall (2007) for further information on this hierarchy of cognitive processing.

It is beneficial to allow your pupils thinking time, regardless of their level, when you have asked a question. This will give them a chance to process the information in order to give you the best answer possible.

brilliant tip

One way to make questioning less threatening for pupils is to say their name first and then ask the question. This will allow them the chance to listen to the question really well, because if they haven't done that, and they therefore can't answer, they could feel humiliated.

Self-assessment

It is important for the pupils to be aware of their own progress. If a pupil knows they are learning successfully in your lessons, they will develop confidence and will be encouraged to take risks with their learning. For example, if they know they have a deep understanding of the material, they will be able to try to apply that knowledge to other situations. If a pupil realises that they have got a bit confused about the work, they will be able to address this by talking to you and their friends, or by consulting books or the Internet in order to be able to correct themselves.

The simplest form of self-assessment is for you to go through the answers at the end of an activity so the pupil knows whether or not their own answers are right. However, even for very young pupils, we can make it much more sophisticated than that, using the National Curriculum level descriptions. These can be found on the Qualifications and Curriculum Development Agency (QCDA) website listed in Appendix 4. They tell you what the pupil should be able to do at each level. You can share these with the pupils (possibly adapting the language into 'pupil-speak'), so they know which levels they are working towards. For example, for a certain piece of work, you will have informed them 'To achieve a level 3, you will …'.

A strong self-assessment exercise is to allow pupils access to the level descriptions and then to set them a question, asking them to answer it in a low-level way and then in a higher-level way, to get them to think about the difference between the two.

brilliant tip

It is worth checking with the class teacher to see if they have some pre-prepared levelled resources that you can use with the pupils. If not and you make some that show pupils the differences between each level, they will be grateful to use them in the future.

Peer assessment

Peer assessment can be a more enjoyable and sometimes more effective way of pupils assessing their own work, through the medium of assessing another's. They could play a game whereby one pupil has to read out the definition and the other has to guess the word. It could really spark an argument, but if it makes them get the book out to see the proper definition, or check with you, they will have learned from it. It's a way of highlighting things that they didn't realise they didn't know. When they have to learn the difference between two things, for example prime numbers and composite numbers, they could play 'Snap'; if they both put down a card showing a prime number, they have to say 'Snap', or if they both put down a card showing a composite number, they say 'Snap'.

You could plan an activity for assessment for learning in groups, where you set up a multiple choice quiz, with each question clearly labelled with the level or grade it is. If the team chooses a level 3 question and they get it right, they get 3 points. If a team chooses a level 2 question, which they are more likely to get right, they only get 2 points. In a competition situation, the pupils will be more likely to want to get it right and they will confer before giving the answer. They will also think about how confidently they would be able to answer questions at different levels. If the pupils' answers are assessed by another group, both groups will be thinking deeply about what constitutes an answer at that level or grade.

Marking other pupils' work

It is valuable for pupils to mark each other's work. This gives them a critical eye that they may not have tuned into! As long as you establish rules and boundaries about using positive language (no put-downs, only constructive advice, you must say at least two positive things), pupils tend to be quite sensitive. When they are thinking about ways in which other pupils could improve their work, they are also thinking about whether or not they did that and wondering what people might say about theirs. Sometimes, the opinions of other pupils can actually be more effective than the teacher's! Because of this, before you get pupils to mark each other's work, it would be beneficial to have a class discussion about what would make a good piece of work. For example, make sure they know the kind of facts and understanding you are looking for.

Another good form of peer assessment is to get the pupils to mark each other's tests, using either the standard mark scheme, or for younger pupils, a mark scheme in 'pupil-speak'. This could be done with two pupils sitting together and marking the tests together, or by them swapping tests and marking them individually. It is an excellent way to get pupils used to the kind of language and detail that is expected for higher levels and also shows that there are no unknown factors in achieving these levels. Of course, you should mark the test afterwards. We have to accept that pupils are highly influenced by social factors when they are at school and may not be totally impartial. To add to that, every time I undergo this process, although pupils try to be accurate, I have to add or remove a small number of marks. It is important to assess accurately because our future lessons depend on our analysis at this point.

brilliant tip

If you are getting pupils to mark each other's tests, it is a good idea to get them to write 'marked by ...' followed by their name on the paper they are marking. This will highlight the fact that it will be noticed and there will be consequences if they try to do their friend a favour by giving them extra marks. You should also ensure that a different coloured pen is used, so they are not tempted to change an answer after seeing the mark scheme.

brilliant example – peer assessment

Mr Jones wanted to familiarise his pupils with some of the English APP criteria. At the start of the lesson, he explained his thinking and gave the pupils the objectives: 'to practise recalling information from text, to recall as much information as you can and to level another pupil's ability to recall'. He displayed some 'pupil-speak' versions of the criteria on the board, showing clearly what the pupils had to do to accomplish each level.

Mr Jones then gave the pupils enough time to read the text and got them to work in pairs, with each person having a copy of the 'pupil-speak' criteria in front of them. He then asked the pupils to interview each other about the text, listening carefully to the answers to try to decide what level their partner is working at. At the end, he gave each pupil a sheet, asking them to fill in the name of the person they interviewed and what impressed them. There were also sections to be completed asking which level the interviewer thought their partner was working at and what they would need to do to move up to the next level.

By the end of the lesson, the pupils did not necessarily get all of their level judgements correct, but they gained a deeper understanding of what was required to attain higher levels and of the way the teachers assess them. This built their confidence to ask how to improve their work in subsequent lessons.

Effective feedback

AfL is not about marking and grading a test or bookwork. Pupils are able to gauge from this kind of feedback only what they got, but are powerless to improve. We often

> AfL is about giving pupils an opportunity to learn more

think that if a pupil gets a grade lower than expected, they need to revise more, but maybe they need tips on how to revise more effectively. A pupil can use a test as an actual learning exercise if you mark it, make suggestions for improvement, and then give the pupil a chance to improve it. AfL is about giving pupils an opportunity to learn more, after they have found out what they need to be able to do that. This sounds like a lot of work, but if you get pupils to make amendments to work in a different coloured ink, it actually takes a very small amount of time to re-mark. This type of activity significantly increases their feeling of empowerment and motivation.

brilliant tip

Something that maintains motivation is to return pupils' work, together with their assessed grade and targets for improvement, while it is still fresh in their memory, i.e. quickly! They are more likely to see their work as important if you do too!

The feedback you provide needs to be very clear about how to improve their work. For many teachers, it is tempting to write targets such as 'Don't mess around in class' or 'Listen better in class', which are understandable, but there are other means to communicate this. It is inappropriate to write it at the end of a formal piece of work. It would be more useful to write something about how to answer the questions, such as letting pupils know the difference between 'describe' and 'explain', or 'When there are two points for the question, you will need to make at least two statements'. Of course, just as constructive would be to tell them things they need to revise more or learn for the first time if there is no evidence of it, such as 'Learn how to expand the brackets'. The most effective next step is then for the pupil to take your advice and produce a piece of work to prove that they have made those improvements.

With the more formal APP, depending on how you have planned the opportunity for your pupils to meet the criteria, the pupils may be able to bring their work up to you during the lesson. If you have familiarised yourself with the level descriptions, or have them printed in front of you, you could feed back with 'This is currently a level 3. To make it a level 4, you need to …' Pupils will usually grasp this chance and come straight back as soon as they have followed your suggestions.

AfL is a very important tool for building pupils' awareness of their own learning and this naturally leads to them taking more responsibility for it. It is extremely rewarding when a pupil asks if they can do a piece of work again and brings it back a level higher, because they have chosen to improve their grade. This kind of positive learning environment is something all teachers should encourage. It is a way of you and the pupil working together to reach a shared goal.

brilliant dos and don'ts

Do

✔ Do build assessment for learning into every single lesson. Otherwise, you won't know if it is appropriate to assume knowledge and move on.

✔ Do use methods in lessons that give you an answer from every single pupil. Asking questions and allowing the same few pupils to answer every time only gives you an understanding of those pupils' abilities.

Don't

✘ Don't rely solely on bookwork to assess progress. Remember, pupils often copy each other!

✘ Don't let a pupil leave the room feeling dejected after achieving a low grade. If you pick up on this, talk to them about things they can do to improve next time. Be prepared to put some time in to help them do this.

✘ Don't rely on target grades and assume that your pupils will be making the appropriate progress. The tests that contributed towards the original target grades may have been taken on a bad day for a pupil. You have to assess constantly to be able to get the most accurate idea of a pupil's capabilities.

brilliant recap

To have a large number of AfL methods and activities at your disposal is crucial, for you and the pupils to know whether or not

▶

appropriate levels of progress are being made and if not, what needs to be done about it. Getting pupils involved in the process and giving them an insight on how their levels of attainment are decided is empowering and motivating for them, shifting them from being passive observers to active learners.

There are a number of ways of assessing progress, from quick in-class methods, to peer and self-assessment processes, to APP, to tests. All of these assessment activities become learning activities if pupils can see how to improve and, even better, if they are given a chance to do so. No matter what level a pupil is achieving, if they are improving, they should be congratulated. Constant assessment allows both you and the learner to track progress to make sure they are always improving their grades and are therefore able to achieve as much as they can.

CHAPTER 9

Meeting individual needs

No two pupils will learn in exactly the same way, but there will be some pupils for whom you will have to make a particular effort to meet their individual needs. These pupils include those with Special Educational Needs (SEN), who demonstrate issues such as:

- learning at a slower pace than others;
- literacy or numeracy difficulties;
- social, emotional or behavioural difficulties.

This is, of course, not a definitive list. In your placement schools, there will be an SEN register. The SEN register will be the responsibility of the Special Educational Needs Coordinator (the SENCo). Your Professional Tutor should set up a meeting between the SENCo and all of the trainee teachers, so they can explain to you how to access the register and how the information is stored. They will also explain confidentiality rules. For example, it is usually inappropriate to discuss the pupils' learning issues in front of other pupils or parents.

The SENCo will tell you how to access the Individual Education Plans (IEPs) for pupils on the register. These documents will be useful **each pupil's needs are different** for you as each one contains information about the aspects of learning that the pupil finds difficult and what you must do to make the curriculum more accessible to them. Taking certain actions to minimise the impact of the pupil's learning needs is sometimes entitled 'differentiation'. It is difficult to outline what this might include, because each pupil's needs are different, but here are some that I have found most common and what you could do to increase the pupil's capacity to learn.

Difficulty with reading

For each age, an expected reading ability has been established and pupils are given a reading age, depending on which age their reading skills correspond to. If the pupil's reading age is significantly lower than their actual age, the school should have in place some extra assistance, in terms of computer programs they can use to practise their reading, or time with Teaching Assistants (TAs). However, there are things you can do to help make your lessons accessible to these pupils.

With some pupils, it might be appropriate to rewrite some materials in simpler words. Some textbook publishers also publish books that look the same as their normal books, but that have bigger writing, with fewer and easier words. These can be given out at the same time as the others, so nobody knows that they are different. It is often preferred by the pupil that their learning difficulties are not highlighted. Sometimes, the difficulty in reading might be helped by just enlarging the text.

If the pupil has dyslexia, research suggests that the words will mix together more on white paper than other colours. The use of cream or 'barley' coloured paper instead of white is thought to reduce this effect significantly. A coloured acetate overlay might otherwise help. If the pupil's reading ability is very low, they may be allowed to have somebody, such as a TA, read text out to them.

 **tip**

Any measures you take to make your lessons more accessible to these pupils must not mean that they will be lost in their exams. Teaching Assistants should only read text out to pupils as a standard course of action if the pupil is allowed somebody to do that for them in their formal assessments. If they are not, then they should still be encouraged to practise reading in lessons.

Difficulties with writing and spelling

If pupils' difficulties in writing and/or spelling cause them problems in understanding the curriculum, there are a number of things you can do. If you are planning a lesson in a subject other than Literacy, it is probably a priority that you ensure that the pupils meet your specific lesson's learning objectives. It is important that their difficulties don't impede their development in other subjects, in which they might be just as good as, or even better than, the rest of the class.

You could help pupils by allowing them to write shorter answers or providing them with what are known as 'cloze' activities. These are sections of text, with gaps for the important new words to be filled in, to check the pupils' understanding of new vocabulary. You could also greatly help pupils by providing them with lists of key words for every topic, along with their meanings. These could be kept in the backs of their books, so they can always refer to them. You should also have new words for each lesson written on the board, to stay there throughout the lesson, which would be useful for all pupils. It is also found to be beneficial if key words are displayed around the room on posters, so pupils can always check their spelling.

If the pupils' difficulties with writing are slowing down their work, to the point that they can't keep up with the rest of the class, or demonstrate their ability in the subject you are teaching, it might be appropriate for a TA to do the writing for them while they dictate. It is important if this step is taken that the TA really does write what the pupil says word for word and doesn't add any of their own words. Otherwise, you wouldn't be able to assess your pupil's ability accurately.

Difficulty with numeracy

In some primary schools and most secondary schools, pupils will be placed into ability sets for Mathematics or Numeracy and Literacy or English. This goes some way to helping to address pupils' needs, as it will prevent a situation where pupils are learning at extremely different paces. However, some pupils' needs will have to be met on an individual basis.

In Mathematics and Numeracy, you may need to provide the pupil with simpler sums, or sums that have some steps already completed, to make calculations less complicated and daunting for the pupil. The pupil might be provided with a calculator, if mental arithmetic is not being assessed. It would also be valuable to provide learners with times tables grids, which will make some of the multi-stage sums more accessible. Another aspect of Numeracy pupils find difficult is the drawing of graphs. If you are assessing the plotting of the points, rather than the ability to draw the whole graph, it would be good to provide them with a sheet with the axes pre-drawn and numbered. It might be useful to provide the pupil with squared paper, maybe with larger squares, so the calculation or diagram can be bigger, which might make it easier to process mentally.

brilliant tip

Always keep in focus what you need the pupil to achieve during the lesson. As long as intervention does not contradict the learning objectives, it is acceptable to cut out unnecessary steps that you will not be assessing, to help speed things up for the pupil. However, it is important to remember that you will have some responsibility for developing their Literacy and Numeracy skills throughout your time with them.

Physical needs

You might have a pupil with a physical need in your class. Of course, this will not mean that their speed or depth of learning is affected, but you will need to make special considerations. For example, it might be a sight issue or that they can't move around the class in the same way as other pupils. Some will be constantly accompanied by a TA, who will fetch resources for them so they don't need to move around as much, or read materials to them. Some will be provided with a laptop computer or Dictaphone if they are unable to write. You really must speak to the class teacher or read their IEP to find out exactly what you need to do to help and what you need to avoid, as well as what to do if they display certain symptoms as a result of their disability that are cause for concern. Also make sure the pupil knows to ask you if they need help with something. Other pupils are generally very helpful towards pupils with disabilities.

brilliant tip

Especially before your first few lessons, discuss with the class teacher any actions you intend to take to assist your SEN pupils. Their experience will help you to make sure that what you have planned is appropriate.

Difficulties in specific subjects

If a pupil has a special educational need in a particular subject, you need to allow them to progress their learning in small manageable chunks during those lessons, and help them to assess their learning regularly, so you both know if they are on track to make good progress. Have regular contact with them throughout the lesson to get them on to the next step towards improvement. It is important to be aware that they might not work as fast as other pupils and not push them too hard, and certainly not get frustrated with them.

When you are holding class discussions, allow all pupils opportunities to succeed. Refrain from asking pupils questions at a much higher level than their current ability. If they are able to answer questions in class, even if you have deliberately made them short-answer questions or lower-level questions, it will help to build their confidence.

brilliant tip

You might need to give pupils different learning resources. Often, if you do an Internet search, you will find that there are computer programs that will allow your pupils to learn at a differentiated level and that also make learning more enjoyable for them than the worksheets that could so easily daunt them.

Learning styles

provide lots of different ways of learning

One way to help pupils with SEN is to provide them with lots of different ways of learning. Some pupils who find writing or reading difficult might excel at card-sorting activities or modelling activities. Remember to try to make your lessons accessible to everybody in the class. You could also give pupils a choice about how to present their knowledge and skills, which might result in some writing large amounts while others draw annotated diagrams. As long as they are meeting the learning objectives, either is acceptable. See Chapter 7 for more information on this.

Grouping

You could carefully plan groups in your class so that the pupils with SEN work with pupils who do not have such difficulties. You will find that the pupils of higher ability will naturally take over the more difficult tasks and communicate with the rest of the group.

You might also group all of the pupils with similar learning needs together and either provide them with work suitable for pupils working at a lower level or get them to work with a TA. You have to manage this carefully though, so the pupils don't become isolated from the rest of the group. Also, make sure that you are only grouping them according to their ability in that particular task or subject, not their general ability.

brilliant tip

It is encouraging for SEN pupils to provide them with rewards for improving their skills. For example, if they can spell three new words by the end of the week, they get a sticker, or merit point, or whatever corresponds to the school's praise system. As these pupils might have low self-esteem, celebrate any achievements, not just those that are knowledge based. For example, if they worked well as a group, that also deserves praise.

Emotional and Behavioural Difficulties (EBD)

Some pupils, for whatever reason, be it a difficult childhood or a physiological or psychological problem, will have difficulties in behaving appropriately. This can manifest itself in all sorts of ways, such as a lack of social skills, aggression, introversion, or even fidgeting. If you are concerned that a pupil might have EBD, ask for the class teacher's advice. Such a pupil might be less responsive to normal praise or disciplinary courses of action.

The ways of dealing with EBD will depend on the individual pupil and what their needs are, but they might include:

● offering rule reminders;

● giving clear instructions and even checking with the pupil that they understand the instruction;

●. remaining calm and refraining from shouting;

● lots of praise and encouragement, although if the pupil doesn't appear to respond well to this, they might not appreciate public attention, so more subtle praise might be required;

● praising behaviours as well as academic achievements;

● seating them away from people with whom they get distracted;

● remaining consistent. Pupils with EBD will need a stable environment.

More tips on behaviour management can be found in Chapter 13.

Gifted and Talented pupils

Gifted and Talented pupils are those who have been identified by at least one teacher as exceptionally able in a particular subject. There are many criteria that could have led to this identification, such as being in the top 5 per cent of the year group or simply standing out as much more able than other pupils. They do not have to be gifted in all subjects to be part of the school's Gifted and Talented programme and it could just be one skill. Your school will have a Gifted and Talented coordinator, who is probably different from the SENCo and whom you will also be able to meet. They will be responsible for putting together a calendar of enrichment activities to inspire these pupils and take them onto a higher level than normal lessons might achieve. The activities might not be curriculum based, but could be vocational. For example, in one school where I have worked, one of the activities was to work with the local BBC branch, to write and present a news story.

If the pupil is Gifted and Talented in a subject or lessons that you are teaching, it is also your responsibility to ensure that they are allowed to reach their potential, by providing them with stimulating and extensive learning activities. They might find what you plan for other pupils relatively easy and could get bored quickly, so you have to keep them interested. It's not just about learning more, it's about learning to a greater depth and a higher level of complexity. After all, they might be the experts of the future.

brilliant tip

Gifted and Talented students might ask questions that you can't answer. It is important that you don't mistake this as a challenge to your own ability or authority. If you don't know the answer, it's fine to explain that, to try to work it out yourself and to take them through those steps you are using to work it out. Otherwise, ask them to see if they can find out using books or the Internet and keep checking with them to see if they can teach you something about it.

Things that you can do to help your Gifted and Talented pupils succeed include:

● setting up revision cards with questions on one side and answers on the other for them to either practise or add to themselves;

- allowing them to go to a section of subject-related magazines or books to read through as they wish when they have completed the tasks;

- allowing them to go to a pile of *interesting* worksheets or activities (such as relevant card games);

- helping other pupils – it sounds like a copout, but teaching someone else about things encourages people to process information more deeply and check their own understanding;

- throwing a thought-provoking question out to the class, without taking immediate answers, to allow the pupils to ponder it and discuss it with you during the lesson.

brilliant tip

Some pupils will be wary of appearing to be too clever and being labelled as a 'boffin', so be sensitive. Make sure you praise all pupils, no matter what their achievements, and avoid praising only the higher-level pupils.

Leave your extension activities in a place in your room familiar to the pupils, so they won't feel embarrassed by having to come and ask you for more work. Or, write the instructions on the board, so pupils will start it as soon as they have finished their other work.

You could set your Gifted and Talented pupils up on a project, either together or individually. Make it relevant to modern life, so they know how this subject actually affects our lives and the world. It could involve links to organisations that are willing to work with schools, for example with communication by e-mail. It could even involve video conferencing with organisations or other schools, either in your country or somewhere else in the world. If you set it up well and communicate it clearly, the Gifted and Talented pupils will be able to work on it without your direction if they finish the other classwork early, or if you know that they already understand what you would like to spend the lesson teaching.

brilliant tip

It is important that you make any extension activities stimulating, so the pupils will want to do them. To just give them more of the same isn't very encouraging and won't necessarily extend their learning.

Empowering all pupils

All pupils will benefit from learning materials that clearly state what needs to be done for each level to be achieved. They will then decide which level they are most comfortable working towards. Of course, you will need to ensure that this is similar to their target grade and, if not, give them positive encouragement to aim higher, with guidance. See Chapter 8 for more information on this.

A positive learning environment

Make sure you celebrate all achievement, even if it is less than you had hoped for. Pupils are more likely to take risks, even when they are aware

create a positive learning environment

of their personal difficulties, if they do not feel threatened. It is essential that you create a positive learning environment.

Differentiation by outcome

I have read many lesson plans in which the differentiation section is filled in with the phrase 'Differentiation by outcome'.

This means that the pupils' achievements will be different. There are some situations in which you can do very little to help the pupils with SEN, and you will have to accept that therefore the outcomes will be different. However, be careful not to fall into the trap of writing this in every lesson plan. It doesn't help the pupils and if you are just doing it to tick a box on the lesson plan, the teacher will notice.

Teaching Assistants

It is valuable for pupils and for you if you develop a relationship with your TA in which you both know what to do to help the pupil and so they can use their own initiative. They need to be well directed and it is important for you to think about what you would like them to be doing during each activity. There is more information about working with TAs in Chapter 14.

Please remember ...

Either having SEN or being Gifted and Talented can lead to frustration on the pupils' part, which is unsatisfactory. It is also disadvantageous for you, because it can easily lead to distracting behaviour, stemming from their boredom, which will have a negative impact on your lesson.

 brilliant dos and don'ts

Do

✔ Do plan to accommodate for SEN and Gifted and Talented pupils. It is important that your lessons are enjoyable and accessible to everybody.

✔ Do be positive and encouraging to all pupils, especially those with learning needs and EBD, so they know when they have achieved something to be proud of.

✔ Do be particularly patient with pupils with EBD. They might have those difficulties for a reason and need your support.

Don't

✘ Don't use the phrase 'Differentiation by outcome' on every lesson plan. It can come across as thoughtless and could be taken to mean that you haven't considered how you are going to meet individual needs.

✘ Don't make it obvious to the rest of the class that some pupils have SEN, especially EBD.

✘ Don't ignore the Gifted and Talented pupils – they are people who could potentially have a large impact on the world in the future!

brilliant recap

Your class will probably contain some SEN pupils and some Gifted and Talented pupils. Although it is easier to plan your lesson for the pupils who will make an 'average' amount of progress, it is important to provide for all pupils, so they can achieve as much as they are able. There are countless numbers of types of SEN and they are in fact individual, so you might encounter some that are not detailed in this chapter. It is therefore important to read IEPs every year, as pupils' needs change throughout the course of their education, and to be creative in your ways of helping them. You could even set up a dialogue with the pupil about what they would find useful.

To create the best learning environment, it is essential that you are positive about all achievements and that you allow pupils to feel empowered, by making it clear what they need to do to improve. It is also imperative that you establish an organised working relationship with the TAs, so you can make the most of their time in your classroom. If you successfully cater for the needs of all pupils in your class, you will significantly reduce the likelihood of disruptive behaviour, caused by boredom or frustration.

CHAPTER 10

E-learning

E -learning is the term given to the use of Information and Communication Technology (ICT), to aid learning. It includes the use of ICT by pupils, or the teacher using ICT to assist or enhance pupils' education. E-learning was just becoming a tool for teaching and learning as I entered the career. I had to reserve the projector and used it to show animations that helped to explain scientific concepts, such as the path of oxygen through the lungs and around the body. The pupils would watch in amazement. Of course, they're used to it now and I can't think of a lesson in which I don't use e-learning to some extent, but it is still just as engaging. On the Internet, or on computer software, or on things you have been able to plan in advance, you can have more detailed, better diagrams, movement and colour – all of which is a big improvement on what somebody can draw on the board during the lesson. Its use helps us to account for the fact that there are likely to be more visual learners in our classes than auditory or kinaesthetic (see Chapter 7).

Nowadays, it is quite usual for a classroom to be fitted with an LCD projector. I hope for your sake that this is the case in your placement

the uses of e-learning are growing in number

schools, because it saves a lot of time. The uses of e-learning are growing in number and the more creative you are, the more you'll find. Here are some examples of the use of e-learning to facilitate education (you'll find useful web addresses in Appendix 4).

Teacher-led activities

Animations

To get an animation about anything, just go onto a search engine and type in 'animation + [subject]'.

Video clips

Projecting video clips is also e-learning. The BBC website in particular has excellent video clips from various series. Pupils particularly like clips from current or recent television programmes. This is a good way of keeping your lessons relevant to modern life. Of course, there are many websites that contain video clips. Just type 'video + [subject]' into a search engine.

brilliant tip

All video clips will need to be vetted for content and language before they are played! It is also useful to play them through once before the start of the lesson and keep the webpage open to prevent streaming problems.

Sometimes, we watch a film and notice a clip that would be particularly effective in demonstrating something or inspiring the pupils, but we don't want to risk the pupils seeing other parts of it, inappropriate for any reason. There now exist several pieces of software that will capture sections of a DVD or video clip that you are playing through your computer. Ask the ICT technician what programs your placement school already has.

Class quizzes

There are many already prepared quizzes online at your disposal, on education websites. There are other websites, such as the TES website, that contain downloadable games, written by other teachers who have kindly uploaded them at no cost. These are sometimes the best because experienced teachers will have designed them, knowing what works well. You can set the class up in teams, or have a running championship, either for individuals or groups. To add to this, you can use computer programs, such as PowerPoint; when pupils click on their multiple choice answer, it takes them to a 'correct' or 'incorrect' slide. Even better, if the answer is incorrect, that slide could contain weblinks to revision pages for them to read, to be able to go back and do the test again, this time getting all the answers correct. Introducing a competitive element is very good at attracting the attention of the more extrovert individuals and can help to make the lesson fun.

Data-logging

Using data-logging to take measurements is great e-learning. This is where you take measurements and readings digitally, so those results can be downloaded onto a computer and manipulated statistically or graphically.

Interactive whiteboards

Interactive whiteboards are highly respected tools for e-learning. However, they can be difficult to synchronise perfectly, or they may need to be re-synchronised regularly. Also, once a pupil is up at the board trying to do things on it, they create a shadow which means that either they, or the rest of the class, can't see what they're doing. However, the programs they come with are excellent. You can:

- move pictures around;
- move labels to pictures, after being directed by the pupils;

- annotate pictures or writing;
- rotate or mirror image pictures;
- record what you have just done to play back;
- get the pupils to explore interactive animations;
- get the pupils to link word boxes with their definitions.

An alternative to an interactive whiteboard is a small, robust electronic board that you can pass to pupils to write on with the accompanying electronic pen, or to use the pen as a mouse, whereby whatever they do is projected on the board. So, you can get pupils to draw or write something on the board from their seats. You can get them to write calculations or anything you could do with a normal mouse, but slightly easier and because you're getting the pupil to do it rather than you, it becomes an assessment for learning exercise (see Chapter 8), where other pupils could comment on the answer or vote for 'correct' or 'incorrect'. This is good for engaging the pupils, especially when you have already been talking to them for a while. These pieces of equipment have various names depending on the manufacturer, for example 'Classpad', 'Drawing Tablet' or 'Interactive Slate'.

Electronic voting pads

One particularly enjoyable branch of e-learning is electronic voting. If you provide pupils with an electronic voting pad each, you can put multiple choice questions on the board and they each vote on their voting pad. You instantly find out which person got the answer right first and the students are informed immediately on their pad whether or not their answer was correct. You can play it in a game format where their characters race, their speed depending on how many questions they get right and how quickly. The pupils will be engrossed. You can also write your own questions requiring numerical answers for them to send their answers to your computer and again, these can be played in a game format.

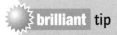 **tip**

E-learning resources are being developed all the time. Speak to the ICT technicians to see what resources are available at your school and to find out about the booking systems.

Pupil activities

Of course, some of the interactive activities above may involve just one or two pupils at a time. To ensure full class participation, there are a number of ways in which you could plan the use of e-learning tasks in your lessons for pupils to undertake at their own pace and even at their own level. This would require at least one computer between two pupils, but it is often best if one computer per person is available. Thankfully, this is a provision in an increasing percentage of schools.

Interactive animations

Some of the animations you find will be interactive, whereby the pupil has to do something correctly for the animation to move on to the next step. The pupil can work through these, learning or revising, and with some they can then use the interactive capabilities to test their knowledge.

Activities made by you

There are many computer programs available now for teachers to be able to set up interactive assessment activities, suitable for testing everything you have taught during the lesson or in the past few lessons. They will then provide instant feedback to the pupils and some even provide the teacher with results on a whole class or individual basis.

Games

There are lots of websites designed for use by teachers that contain games to test pupils' knowledge. They are an enjoyable way for pupils to assess their progress.

Online formal assessment

There are some websites for which your school may have bought a licence to use that will set formal tests for your pupils to sit online. Their results will be calculated and some provide formative feedback. That is, advice to the pupils on how or what to improve. You will be able to log on to get the results, with either a National Curriculum level or a Key Stage 4 grade. The best websites will then give you a breakdown of which questions were answered most successfully, in order for you to know what needs to be revised. Some schools use the results from these programs to help form their Teacher Assessment grades.

Differentiation

The beauty of setting e-learning tasks for your pupils is that you are able to set different tasks for different pupils. On some activities, pupils could be working at different levels from each other. There are even some websites designed to be used by pupils with Special Educational Needs (see Chapter 9).

Learning Platforms and Virtual Learning Environments

Schools are now starting to use Learning Platforms and Virtual Learning Environments. These are websites that are used as a learning network by members of the school community – teaching staff, pupils, parents and carers. They can be logged onto from school or home, by any of the users.

Teachers can upload their resources onto these websites, so pupils have access to revisit them whenever they wish. It also means that parents or carers are able to see what their children are learning.

> parents or carers are able to see what their children are learning

Teachers can set homework tasks for their classes, with deadlines for their completion, after which time the website will not accept submissions. This saves administration time for the teacher and it means that the information can be accessed from any Internet connection, with a username and password. Of course, this system also means that parents can monitor whether or not their children are completing their homework, because there will constantly be an up-to-date record online. Virtual Learning Environments and Learning Platforms can also be used by all people involved to monitor performance, attendance, punctuality, and behaviour and achievement records.

brilliant tip

If you are working with a class whose teacher does not often use e-learning, don't be put off using it yourself. Seeing the enthusiasm from the pupils might encourage the teacher to use it more and they may learn some techniques from you.

brilliant dos and don'ts

Do

✔ Do ask other members of staff if you are struggling to find an e-learning resource that you are sure must be available. The chances are that they have searched for it too and they may have been successful.

▶

✔ Do keep an organised record of your e-learning resources. Save web addresses on 'Favourites', preferably organised into year group or topic folders. Download activities if it is an option because it is very frustrating to search for an excellent website that you used last year, only to find that it is no longer there.

✔ Do check e-learning resources before you use them. Because technology is constantly changing, you cannot expect your Internet-based resources to be the same as they were last time. Methods of login and the organisation of resources on the Internet change frequently.

Don't

✘ Don't ignore technophobia. If you dislike using computers to the point that you will either ignore them as a possibility or will feel stressed by e-learning, make sure you let your Mentor know that you will need some training. It is likely that e-learning will become even more embedded into teaching practice in future, so face your fears now!

 **brilliant** recap

The term e-learning encompasses all sorts of activities, from dragging labels to appropriate parts of diagrams, to interactive animations, to games, to formal assessment. It is becoming an increasingly integral part of teaching and learning. It is a well-enjoyed aspect of lessons for pupils and has made many concepts and ideas more accessible for them.

Some people do not feel confident with the use of e-learning in their lessons, but it is important to get to grips with it, because it cannot be ignored and will not go away. It is important to ensure that you have been trained sufficiently to be able to use e-learning in your teaching and to remain organised, so you will know how to access your favoured e-learning resources quickly. That way, you will find it easier to work with the ever more popular Virtual Learning Environments and Learning Platforms and will be able to use them to their full potential.

CHAPTER 11

Lesson
planning

esson planning is a good way of taking you through the steps necessary to be able to deliver an effective lesson. In order to command respect as somebody who knows how to provide a high-quality education, you need to know exactly what you are doing from the very start of the lesson.

It's hard to act assured, but when you have planned a lesson well, pupils pick up on your confidence subconsciously. Things will come naturally that you can't possibly concentrate on for the whole of the lesson, like tone of voice, facial expression, body language, the fact that everything is to hand immediately and there is no hesitation. All of these things make the pupils feel as though they are in safe hands.

In addition to this, lesson planning is one of the opportunities you have to exercise some creativity. If you plan an activity they weren't expecting, one that gets pupils up and moving around the room, or working in groups, or if you have found an excellent video clip or animation to illustrate a point, they will really appreciate it and be much more likely to remember the lesson.

When you have delivered a good lesson, when the pupils have really learned and you have done your job well, you can't help but feel great about it. A casual statement such as 'I enjoyed that lesson, Miss', or 'that was fun', can make all the preparation worthwhile.

What it needs to contain

Here follows a list of things that should be included in your lesson plan. It guides you through the thought processes that should take place for you to be able to deliver a successful lesson.

Objectives

You need to know in advance exactly what you expect the pupils to learn from that lesson. Of course, some may exceed this and ask for more information, or some may struggle slightly. If you have set clear objectives, you will be able to compare your pupils' performance to what you hoped for and use this for the evaluation of your lesson and of their learning.

> setting objectives is very important

Setting objectives is very important and you will be expected to do it for every lesson. You should have the learning objectives up on the board at the very start. The following are example formats:

- Objectives: to be able to describe ...
- Objectives: to know what is needed for ...
- Objectives: to find out ...
- Objectives: to be able to explain why ...
- Objectives: to be able to write a list of ...
- Objectives: to carry out an investigation to find out ...
- Objectives: to understand the necessity for ...
- Objectives: to understand why some people feel that ...

It is useful for pupils to know in advance what they are meant to be learning. They are fully aware that sometimes teachers drift off and talk about other things, as an aside, or to elaborate on a point. We should allow them the opportunity to hear certain things and think 'right, really concentrate now'. They will also use the objectives when you have set them tasks to complete, so they know they're on the right track.

Have you ever read a book where there seem to be chapters on which you can't place any significance? Of course, you may understand the relevance by the end, but for a brief moment you think 'What is the point of this?', 'Where is this going?' This same feeling can be very frustrating in lessons. For this reason, pupils not only need to have the objectives made clear at the start, but the teacher needs to refer to them regularly throughout the lesson. For example:

- 'Of course, these kinds of describing words are exactly what you need to be able to meet the objectives of this lesson.'

- 'This is all helping us to learn which is fastest, which is what the lesson is about.'

- 'Remember to be thinking about the list you need to have written by the end of the lesson.'

brilliant tip

It can be useful to get pupils to copy the objectives into their books as soon as they come into the room. This can be used as a way of establishing a habit, to switch them into lesson mode and to encourage them to forget about what they had been doing at break time. However, it does also mean that they have the objectives in their books throughout the entire lesson, which means they cannot forget them. In addition, it means that if they revise from their books, they have a guide to remind them what they should have learned.

Outcomes – a better alternative?

Some people believe that 'outcomes' is a preferred alternative to 'objectives'. This is because many teachers, when writing their objectives, pretty much write in that one sentence what the pupils need to have learned by the end of the lesson, such as 'to know that the energy required for photosynthesis comes from the Sun'. Understandably, this leads some pupils to think 'Well, if I know that now, what is the point of being in the lesson?' An alternative 'outcome' would be 'to have used experimental evidence to find out where the energy for photosynthesis comes from'. Outcomes need to cover what the pupils will have done by the end of the lesson, as well as what they will have learned. Some pupils find outcomes like this easier to 'tick off' mentally, like a list of tasks. Your objectives or outcomes should be at the start of every lesson plan.

Timing

> it is important to know how long each activity you have planned will take

It is important to know how long each activity you have planned will take. This prevents you from spending too much time on particular tasks and ensures that what you have planned will fit into the lesson. Your timing also needs to allow for the fact that it takes a few minutes for pupils to enter the room, get their equipment out and settle down. You need to include the time it takes to do the register and to pack any equipment away at the end. Sticking to your planned timing helps you to remain in control of the pace of the lesson and stops you from being in an absolute fluster at the end of it. It also prevents the class teacher from feeling that they should step in to finish the lesson on time.

If you realise your activity is over-running, bring it to a close, or think about which activities you can drop or shorten later on. Thinking these things through prevents that embarrassing moment of the bell going while you are halfway through doing something. Because, then, some pupils will not have the manners to stay seated silently and might start packing away. Then, you will have the job of settling the class down again so you can continue. Timing is the key to ending a lesson in a controlled, calm, professional manner.

Starters, main activities and plenaries

This is a commonly used structure to a lesson. It means that pupils are introduced to the lesson, its relevance to the current topic and maybe life in general. It then guides the pupil through the new learning. At the end of the lesson both you and the pupils should have an idea of whether they have learned what they were supposed to learn.

Starter

Reluctant as I am to admit having watched Australian soaps (come on – I grew up in the eighties!), I have to acknowledge the use of their sections at the beginning of each episode, which recap the last or last few episodes. It's all about reminding the audience of what they already know and getting them into the frame of mind of wanting to know what happens next.

The starter of a lesson has exactly that purpose. You don't always have to remind pupils of what they already know, although it is often a useful exercise, but your starter definitely needs to be an activity that makes the pupils want to learn what you are about to teach them.

Starters could be:

- watching a video clip, followed by a 'what happens next?' discussion;
- showing pupils a piece of equipment and asking 'What could this be used for?';
- finding out what the pupils have retained from the last lesson, through the use of an Assessment for Learning activity (see Chapter 8);

- displaying some pictures and asking pupils to work in pairs to discuss what they all have in common;
- getting pupils to sort some cards into the right order;
- anything that intrigues them!

Starters usually last about 5 or probably a maximum of 10 minutes. They are there to set the scene for the lesson.

Main activity

The main activity is where the new learning takes place. It should be the largest part of the lesson. But don't be misled into thinking that this means it can be only one activity. It could be as many as you choose, as long as you have given all pupils the opportunity to meet the learning objectives by the end of the lesson.

Plenary

In every lesson, you need some way of knowing how well the pupils have met the objectives. It is best that this is not just in the form of a question and answer session, especially not if you allow the pupils to volunteer answers, because that way you will only gauge the understanding of the confident ones. You can be quite inventive in finding out answers to questions from all pupils in one go. See Chapter 8 for some ideas.

The plenary was traditionally put at the end of a lesson. It was there to round up a lesson and find out how well the pupils have progressed. However, if your school is quite forward thinking, they may not force you to have an end-of-lesson plenary. The main role of the plenary, to assess progress, could actually be appropriate at various stages of the lesson and such assessment could occur more than once. After all, if you gain this valuable information earlier in the lesson, it gives you a good chance to adjust your lesson accordingly.

VAK learning

Try to plan activities to accommodate the different learning styles (visual, auditory and kinaesthetic – see Chapter 7), so that the lesson is accessible to all learners. Remember, you want your lesson to be one that they will remember forever. If you allow them to learn in the way their brains find easiest, this is more likely to happen.

> plan activities to accommodate the different learning styles

 **brilliant** tip

It might be useful for you to have on your lesson plan template tick boxes for V, A and K, to make sure you have included all three.

Meeting individual needs/differentiation

In your class, there will be some pupils who find the work you give to all of the other pupils challenging. This could be due to eyesight issues, dyslexia, or many other reasons. There will also be some that find it too easy (Gifted and Talented). Either scenario can lead to frustration on the pupils' part, which is unsatisfactory and could lead to disruptive behaviour. There is more information on how to make your lessons understandable and productive for pupils with Special Educational Needs and Gifted and Talented pupils in Chapter 9. Have a section in every lesson plan in which you write what you will do for these pupils.

Resources needed

For any practical lessons, I would suggest that lessons are planned at least a week in advance, because you will need to show the plan to the class teacher and give enough notice when handing in a requirements list to technicians. In addition, if you have prepared cards to sort, for example, you may need to get them photocopied and laminated first. Allow people enough time to do it!

✳ brilliant tip

It's wise to have a small space on your lesson plan for evaluation. Something like 'Some pupils found the language too challenging', 'Doesn't help the less confident pupils', 'More explanation needed next time', or sometimes, in my case 'What were you thinking? Never do that again!' That way, you won't make the same mistake next year.

Appendix 2 is an example of a lesson plan, but your placement school may have a preferred structure.

Organisation

From day one at your placement school, every lesson plan should be stored in a folder on your computer titled with the name of the module you are teaching. In Design and Technology, one example would be 1B – Playgrounds. Store that folder in the 'Design and Technology' folder. That should be in the 'Lesson Plans' folder. So, you know that to get to that lesson plan, you have to go to:

- My Documents
  - Lesson Plans
    - Year 1
      - Design and Technology
        - 1B – Playgrounds

You should also, in 'My Documents', have a 'Lesson Resources' folder. This will contain hours of your work. If you do this, next year, when you come to plan a similar lesson, although it cannot be exactly the same because it will depend on the pupils in your class, you can consult the resources folder for ideas, which will save you a lot of time. The resources that you make may be just as useful next year as they are now.

Websites

You should set up a similar system for your Internet Favourites. Every time you find a good website, store it in your Favourites. You just have to click on the '+' sign at the top of the page. When you are in the 'Add to favourites' box, click on 'New folder'. Then do the same. Create a year folder, then, within that, create a folder for the topic or module you are working on. Otherwise, expect to do all that searching again next year!

brilliant dos and don'ts

Do

✔ Do plan all of your lessons. It really will make your teaching more successful.

✔ Do consult your records for the preferred learning styles of pupils in the class. This will have to be considered when planning the most appropriate activities.

✔ Do evaluate your lessons. It's very frustrating when an activity goes wrong and then you remember that it went wrong last time you tried it, too.

Don't

✘ Don't think that once you have delivered a lesson once, you won't have to plan a similar lesson again. Your lesson plan should be based on the pupils you have in your class.

✘ Don't leave copies of your lesson plan hanging around for the pupils to see. It will contain information about SEN.

✘ Don't just use the standard DCSF objectives for your lessons. They might not be in 'pupil-speak'.

 **brilliant** recap

Lesson planning is a time-consuming activity, but a worthwhile one. It takes you through everything you need to think about to be able to deliver a successful lesson, including the phrasing of your objectives, the activities themselves and the information you have available to you to choose the most appropriate ones. It will ensure that you have thought about the resources you will need and the timing. When you have considered all of these points, you will be able to enter the classroom feeling in control and you will be able to spend your energy building positive relationships with your pupils because everything else will be done.

CHAPTER 12

Being observed

You will be observed regularly during your training year. To begin with, you will be observed by the class teachers whenever you teach a lesson or part of a lesson. Your course examiners will need to collect a certain amount of evidence for you to be able to pass the course, including observation forms completed by the class teacher. On all of these forms, there will be a section for them to make notes on what happened, how the pupils responded, what went well and what needs to be improved upon. Qualified teachers are also observed regularly throughout their career and this same format is used.

You can't blame yourself for wanting your lesson to go so perfectly that there are no targets for improvement and I have observed lessons where I have found it difficult to think of one myself. However, the observer isn't really doing their job properly if they don't try to offer any further ideas.

There are certain aspects of teaching, outlined in the 'Professional Standards' (available to view on the TDA website – see Appendix 4), that you must be able to demonstrate to become a Newly Qualified Teacher (NQT). The observation forms that are completed upon your observed lessons will contain a section to highlight which of these Professional Standards you are hoping to exhibit. It is the shared responsibility of you, your Mentor, your Professional Tutor and your training provider to make sure that by the end of the training year, you will have demonstrated every one of those skills at least once, whether in your lessons or in other parts of your school life. Of course, the objective of the training is to get you to a point where you are meeting lots of those standards every lesson (some aren't applicable every time). If, towards the end of the course, there are some standards that you haven't yet met, you will need to ensure that you focus on them.

> the reason for observations is to give you a structure through which to improve

So, the reason for observations is to give you a structure through which to improve and to provide evidence upon which the appropriate authorities can base their judgement. It is perfectly natural to feel nervous on these occasions, but observations are not meant to be threatening experiences. Many teachers will enjoy observing trainee teachers. The training year that you are undertaking is an excellent time to learn the most modern of teaching methods and qualified teachers can learn these from you. Although it is things going wrong that you will dread, the observer will not be looking out only for them; they will be hoping to be impressed. If they have given you some advice during previous feedback sessions, they will be watching to see if you have taken it and will be really pleased if it has worked. Also, remember, they are just people and will have been through this process themselves.

The following section contains tips on how to do well in an observation. Of course, it is ideal if these ideas are used in all of your lessons, but realistically, you really need to pull it out of the bag when you are being formally observed!

How to do well in an observed lesson

Be prepared

Lesson plans

Write your lesson plan in lots of detail, including:

- the date;
- lesson objectives;
- prior learning (what they already know, to show the observer their progression);
- information about Special Educational Needs' requirements and what you have done to address them;
- how you will assess the learning in the lesson;
- how you will address the different learning styles.

For more information on lesson planning, see Chapter 11. Sometimes, a teacher does something that might not look to be appropriately paced or at the appropriate amount of difficulty. If you have lots of detail in your lesson plan, the observer won't be left with too many questions, or get the wrong impression that you haven't thought something through properly.

Resources

Have all of your resources out ready. If you are doing any kind of practical work, where the pupils will need to move around the room to collect resources, spread the resources around, so they will not all crowd in one area, which could lead to disruptive behaviour. If you have any paper materials prepared, have them ready on the desk. You don't want to spend a few minutes looking for them while you are being observed.

Settling pupils down

Have something ready for the pupils to do as soon as they come into the room. This could be a worksheet, or a task written on the board. It will be even easier if you have already got them into this habit of coming in and starting the work immediately. If it's new to them, you might have to shout over them to explain what to do.

Give pupils an unflustered smile and say 'Hello'. You would be best either standing at the door greeting them or at the front of the room, which automatically makes pupils realise that you intend to make an efficient, controlled start. Careful observation of pupils will also allow you the chance to pick up on anything that needs to be dealt with, such as arguments or uniform issues.

Lesson structure

Use PowerPoint or an equivalent presentation program (if you have a projector) to guide you through the structure of the lesson (see Chapter 6 for more information). This will make sure that you don't leave anything out. It could contain the objectives and details of tasks. If they are up on the board, pupils are less likely to ask you over to explain, so you can spend more time assisting them in their learning. The presentation could include questions that you will ask (see Chapter 8 for information on questioning), pictures and links to videos or websites. However, I strongly advise that you have any websites and files that you intend to use already open, so you don't waste time opening them and worse, discovering that they are not working at that time. It also speeds things up to have DVDs pre-loaded at the right place and video clips from the Internet already played through once, to avoid streaming issues.

brilliant tip

You will be expected to be correct in your subject knowledge, so if you are in any doubt that you will remember it, include it in your presentation.

Pace of lesson

include timings for the activities on your lesson plan

All of the above things will increase the pace of the lesson, which is something the observer will be looking for. An appropriately paced lesson will ensure that the pupils don't get time to get distracted and that lots of learning takes place. To help you maintain control over the pace of the lesson, include timings for the activities on your lesson plan.

Meeting individual needs

The observer will be watching to make sure the pupils know what they are supposed to be doing and that their individual needs have been met. See Chapter 9 for more information on this. You will also need to make sure that you have planned the use of any additional staff effectively, to ensure maximum impact on learning. Teaching Assistants could be used to work with small groups of pupils who are struggling to learn as quickly as the rest of the class, or who need the content of the lesson to be extended, or they could work on a one-to-one basis with a pupil with SEN. In any case, they need good direction by you to be of the most use.

brilliant tip

Speak to the TA before the lesson. They are often very sympathetic when we are being observed and although they don't necessarily always have time for it, you could discuss together how best to use their skills.

Group work

Group work is a very good thing to have in your lessons, because pupils learn a lot from each other and it helps us to teach them teamwork skills, so it is recommendable to introduce an activity appropriate for their collaboration. It would be wise to organise this well in advance and, if possible, to have implemented group work tasks in the past. Group work needs to be organised well because if you just ask pupils to work in groups, they will go to work with their friends, which will probably reduce their level of concentration. There might also be arguments if somebody is left out of a group or hurt feelings if one person refuses to work with somebody else. To add to that, the most successful grouping will be decided by you in advance, so each pupil is working in either a mixed ability group or a group with people of a similar ability. Each can be a type of differentiation, but the most appropriate method depends on your lesson objectives. It would then be useful to have the details of the groups up on the board so the groupings are clear to them, as is which desk or area they should go to.

Assessment of progress

It used to be the case that the observer would watch to see what the teacher was doing. This focus has now changed to what the pupils are doing. The teacher could be hugely charismatic with lots of new ideas or less extrovert and using more traditional teaching techniques. If there is evidence during those lessons that progress has been made in the pupils' learning, both lessons might be considered to be successful. It is therefore important to introduce an in-class assessment for learning technique, so progress can be judged (see Chapter 8). Then, if your assessment informs you that the pupils haven't understood as much or as well as expected, or conversely, that they have exceeded your expectations, the observer will be impressed if you react to this to either improve their understanding or push their learning even further. This is a much better way to deal with unexpected results from assessment than to ignore the information, in a determined effort to stick to your lesson plan.

Behaviour

Of course, the observer will be studying the behaviour and attitude of the pupils. However, if you have addressed the above factors well, then the pupils' behaviour should be less of a challenge anyway. If behaviour does become an issue at any time, use non-aggressive means to correct it (see Chapter 13), and if further courses of action are required, stick to the school's policy as usual. The observer will know that sometimes things happen that you weren't able to plan for, but will expect you to deal with them sensibly and calmly.

brilliant tip

The observer will respect you if you are brave enough to use some activities that are potentially brilliant, but are more difficult to control, such as those that involve movement around the room, making models or group work. If these activities don't go as planned, it is fine to suggest to the class that the activity is not going as intended, so you have decided to change to a different activity at this point. It will show far more skill than planning for them to complete questions from a textbook.

Health and Safety

On top of all of this, you will definitely be expected to have carefully planned to maintain the Health and Safety of everybody in the room. As always, you need to make sure you know exactly what to do to make sure everybody is safe if you are using equipment, harmful substances or hazardous movement.

Feedback

At the end of your lesson, or at a later convenient time (which should certainly be within 48 hours), you will need to talk to the observer to receive their feedback. They will tell you whether or not you have met the Professional Standards intended and if not, why not. They will also discuss which parts they thought were successful and which aspects they feel need to be improved. It can be hard to hear the latter, but listening to it will make you a better teacher. If they are down-to-earth people, they will probably

talk to the observer to receive their feedback

admit to you that it doesn't always go to plan for them either and there are also things that they need to work on.

If the observer hasn't spoken to you about the lesson, ask to arrange a time to do so. It is very important to receive this feedback. With regard to their advice for improvement, if you are unsure of what they mean, feel free to ask them to give examples. If they are a teacher in your placement school, you could even ask if they have any lessons coming up in which you might be able to observe them using the skill in question.

If at any time you disagree with the feedback, talk to either the observer, your Mentor or your Professional Tutor about it, if you feel comfortable doing so. Otherwise, contact your Mentor from your training institution, to see what they think. It doesn't have to be a major issue and different teachers operate in different ways. If one observer thinks that you have failed to meet one of the Professional Standards, but you disagree and you happen to also work with another class teacher, it would be worth using this Professional Standard as a focus on a lesson being observed by the other teacher.

brilliant tip

Hopefully, your course providers will have given you a checklist for the Professional Standards, so you are able to track your progress. If not, it might be useful to make one for yourself.

If there are any Professional Standards that you are repeatedly failing to meet, seek all the advice you can get, from the people listed above, but also from fellow trainee teachers and any other teachers in the school. Make sure the teachers you are working with know that it is something you must focus on until you meet the Standard and ask them to discuss with you opportunities that might arise for you to work on it.

brilliant dos and don'ts

Do

✔ Do get pupils into good working habits throughout your time with them, so they are more likely to behave predictably during lessons that are being observed.

✔ Do prepare thoroughly for your lesson, even if you work out that if you spent this much time preparing for every lesson, you'd never sleep! It is worth it to get the feedback on what you are capable of. If you develop the skills now, it won't take you as long in the future.

✔ Do prioritise safety and learning if things don't go to plan. The safety aspect is imperative and if you need to change your lesson plan because what you had planned isn't working, the observer should respect and understand what you are doing. You may need to explain it later, however.

✔ Do try to learn the pupils' names in advance. You need to show the observer that you have been developing positive relationships with them.

Don't

✘ Don't see observations as a negative thing. They are opportunities to show off what you have learned.

✘ Don't tell the pupils in advance that you are being observed and promise them special rewards if they behave well. They might unwittingly mention it in front of the observer and it doesn't look good.

brilliant recap

Being observed can be a stressful experience, but it is important to remember that its purpose is to improve our teaching. The best way to ensure your observation goes well is to prepare well. Have a detailed lesson plan, highlighting prior knowledge, the activities themselves, how you will meet individual needs of pupils and how you will assess their learning.

For your lesson to be successful, you must demonstrate that the pupils are safe, engaged and have made progress. The best way to do the latter is to devise an activity in which the observer can actually see the progress made by all pupils.

PART 4

Classroom management and working with others

CHAPTER 13

Behaviour
management

'm one of those annoyingly optimistic people who think that all pupils are very good people, at least deep down. I believe that bad behaviour comes from a pupil not knowing how to behave well, making genuine mistakes, trying to find their place in society and also from frustration in lessons.

If a pupil is rude to you, don't take it personally. I know it's easy to say, but can you remember a time when you were younger, when you said or did something that you're now ashamed

if a pupil is rude to you, don't take it personally

of or embarrassed about? I know I can and I often ask myself 'What was I thinking?' That is possibly the point. Especially when people are younger, they will say many things without thinking and if they have just offended you, they may look back and cringe at it one day.

To add to that, there is more instinctive behaviour taking place in our classrooms than we care to think about. When pupils come to school, they may see their relationships with their peers to be just as important, if not more so, than their school work. Some of the bad behaviour is just there to impress their friends. Some pupils will want to create for themselves a powerful position, even over you. They may not want to be seen to be submissive and will possibly want to be seen as 'hard'.

On top of all this, pupils will be developing their own thoughts and ideas and may genuinely disagree with you. This is OK.

We should definitely not discourage the courage it takes to go against the norm. If all people grew up or lived their adult lives in accordance with the rules other people set them, there would never be any changes or progress. It is perfectly natural for pupils to question adults and this should not be seen as an insult.

We often expect our pupils to behave better than we do. On non-pupil days, during training sessions, even some teachers will joke with each other and talk over the trainer. I think that we need to have very high expectations of our pupils, but we need to understand that perfect behaviour is a challenge for anyone and we must not resent pupils if they make mistakes.

Some golden rules

1 Treat pupils with respect

Remembering that pupils still have a lot to learn about the appropriate ways to behave helps us to realise what a good role model we should be. So, think about the attributes you would like them to have as adults, and demonstrate those yourself. It is important to be (in no particular order):

- calm
- kind
- polite
- friendly
- forgiving
- sensible
- positive
- caring
- in possession of a good set of morals!

It is surprising how polite pupils will be in response to your own manners. To encourage it, phrases such as 'With those manners, it's a pleasure to help you', 'That's really kind of you, thank you', 'That was very thoughtful, thank you' and 'People in this class have excellent manners' are gratefully received. When they thank you for something, it is good to follow it with some acknowledgement, such as 'You're welcome'.

We can encourage pupils to be polite to each other by giving them the responsibility for it. If there is a situation where pupils are crowding around to get equipment, try saying something like 'I'm so sorry, I haven't kept track of who was first. I would be very grateful if you would be careful to let people through who were here before you'. Seriously, they want to be good people.

2 Don't assume they know

If pupils do something that you find unacceptable, let them know. Something like 'I need to have a rule in this classroom that you only get out of your seats when I give you specific permission, because people find it distracting' will suffice. If they do it again, or in a later lesson, remind them. 'Please remember the rule we have about only getting out of your seats when you have permission.'

3 Have high expectations

We must be certain of our own expectations. Know what kinds of things are so important to you that you will fight for them (of course, I mean in terms of writing letters home, removing privileges, etc.). If you know exactly what you want from a situation, pupils will pick it up through all sorts of subconscious means that you are unaware of. If you are thinking 'They will be silent now', rather than 'OK, I've asked them to be silent – are they going to be? What am I going to do if they're not?', the message will definitely get through. If you are unsure, your voice starts to quiver ever so slightly and your body language may change without you noticing. If you expect pupils to behave badly, they will wonder what is the point of them even trying.

brilliant tip

> Decide what standards of behaviour you expect. For example, when
> they are writing, will you expect silence, quiet talking to those next
> to them, or as much talking as they like? Your decision will come
> across in your teaching.

4 When starting with a new class

When you first meet a class, let them know that you know the
rules already and exactly what the consequences would be if they
were to not follow those rules. It's wise to have definite strategies worked out in advance. They will then get to know that if
they …, then …. Of course, you need to know this too. A good
first statement of authority is to make sure that they are in their
teacher's usual seating plan. Another way of showing the new
class that you have taken control is to stand at the door and
greet pupils.

It is hugely important to be positive,
especially with a new class. Give out
rewards, such as the merit stickers
some schools have if they are the first
to be quiet, or the first to remember to put their hand up, or if
they do something helpful such as give the books out. This lets
them know that it would be good for them if they behave well
for you.

> it is hugely important to
> be positive

5 Use language to demonstrate that you know what you want

Language can be a key to that confident, non-negotiable position. Rather than saying 'Try to leave the room tidy' (allowing
scope for not leaving the room tidy), say 'When you have tidied
up, we'll …' This transmits the fact that it is decided in your
mind that the room will be tidy. Use definite language, like 'We

will', 'Please make sure you', 'When you are', 'While you are doing that, I will ...' and 'As you are ...'. Phrases to avoid when you are giving an instruction include 'If you could ...' and 'Try to ...'.

One really good trick to demonstrate that you do not in any way foresee any issues is to thank pupils immediately, even before they have followed the instruction. 'Take a seat. Thank you', or 'Listening, please. Thank you.' Pupils understand that there will be no arguments if you give them the instruction and move on immediately, not even giving them a chance to do otherwise. So, something like 'Back to your own seat, please. Let Mary sit there. Thank you', followed straight away by 'Hi Chris, how are you getting on?' to the child on the next table confirms that there is no other option. You are not hanging around for them to argue back because you know it's not going to happen. They may grumble under their breath before doing as you have requested, but if it's not offensive, it is often wise to ignore it and let them get it off their chest.

It is possible even to use positive language when telling pupils not to do something. If they are running around, rather than saying 'Stop running', offer them an alternative, preferably with a reason, such as 'Please walk so you don't fall over'.

6 Use visual cues

There are many ways to avoid a confrontation. Rather than saying out loud 'Take your scarf off, please', you could just gesture to the pupil, by removing your imaginary scarf. Hmmm, that is really hard to describe without it sounding like you're going to look ridiculous, but try it, it does work! Another example is if they are talking over you, hold out a blocking hand towards them (kind of like the 'talk to the hand' gesture, but lower and less aggressive). Again, it stops you sounding like a nag.

7 Give them choices

You can make pupils feel empowered and less oppressed by giving them a couple of alternatives to the behaviour you're trying to stop. If a pupil is playing with a toy or mobile phone, your only objective is for them to stop it. So, you could say 'Could that toy either go into your bag or on my desk please?', or, if they're messing around with a fellow pupil, 'I don't think it's wise to sit there. Please sit either …'.

brilliant tip

As long as your objective of correcting the behaviour has been met, it doesn't really matter how the pupil met it. Allow them to have some choice in what they do to solve the problem or improve their behaviour. You could ask them 'What do you think would help you to stay in your seat?'

8 Give them time

It is very rare that a pupil will want to be seen with a 'Yes Miss, right away Miss' attitude. They will appear much cooler if they wait for a few seconds. Allow them this time to follow an instruction. It is their way of sending a message to you and the rest of the class that actually, they don't have to do this, but they are choosing to. As long as your instruction has been followed, you have not lost out.

9 Remind them of the rules

give pupils a chance

Give pupils a chance. If they come into the class noisily, say 'Can I remind you that it's important to come in quietly, so I know you're in the right frame of mind to learn?' They may have actually forgotten or just have been thinking about something else.

10 Explain why you have made the request

Pupils may think you're just being bossy if you don't. It's fine to say 'Could you sit quietly, please? That conversation is putting me off what I'm saying'. Or 'Walk, please, I really don't want you to injure yourselves'.

11 Practise behaviours

Practising behaviours, such as coming into the room sensibly and moving around the room safely, can be productive and can also increase efficiency. It creates neural pathways so the behaviour will eventually become habit.

---

brilliant example

In my Science lessons, sometimes my new classes do not pack away very well at all. So, I tell them that in the next lesson, we'll practise getting equipment out and putting it away sensibly. This may not be part of the originally planned lesson objectives, but is important for the smooth running of subsequent lessons.

---

12 Use humour as a tool for diffusion

This is a way of correcting behaviours without being aggressive. However, you have to be careful who you do this with. It cannot be used with somebody who is particularly sensitive and gets angry easily. You mustn't humiliate your pupils.

After you have asked somebody twice to stop talking over you, it is easy to get angry. Sometimes it helps to stop, look at them with a surprised but smiling expression and say 'Are you actually going to give me a chance to teach here?' The tone of voice can be casual and joking, but you have again let them know that you will not settle for their talking.

 **brilliant** example

I had one pupil making strange grunting noises in my lesson once, just to be disruptive. I said 'Are you OK over there? I'm a bit worried about you. It sounds like you're having a few digestive problems'. The class laughed and the boy stopped.

13 Get to know your pupils

With really difficult pupils, establish something else to talk about with them, rather than just nagging them. It really helps to talk to the class teacher, or other teachers, to find out more about them and to drop this into the conversation.

 **brilliant** example

I found out that one particularly difficult pupil I had liked mountain biking. So, I asked for his advice. It was about something silly like my brakes squeaking, but it showed him that I respected his opinion. I think it helped him to see me as less of a dragon.

14 Follow up everything

You might not be a scary person. Thankfully, you don't need a booming voice for pupils to comply with your instructions and you don't need to tower over them to achieve discipline. Discipline is more effective if it comes from the consistent following up of behaviour issues. If you say you'll set a detention and don't, it's worth the pupils risking it again. If you always apply the consequence you threatened, although it will be hard work to begin with, your reputation for never letting things go will spread and pupils will be reluctant to try messing around, just in case.

15 Make sure pupils know that you're not against them

As you are walking around the room, if you have to address an issue, it really helps to mention something else before you talk about the behaviour. This lets pupils know that you don't see it as a drama. It is even better if you can make a positive comment about their work before you ask them to stop drawing on each other.

If emotions are raised during a discussion, don't rise to it. Don't try to overpower pupils by using a stronger or louder voice. Older pupils especially might reciprocate and somebody will end up losing. They will try very hard to make sure it isn't them. More importantly, pupils need to be able to trust you, rather than fear you.

When you are addressing behavioural issues with pupils, talk about the behaviour and not them. They are not their behaviour and they need to know that you understand that. If someone shouted out in your class, they are not a shouter, but they shouted. If they had one fight, they are not aggressive, but they did get involved in one fight. So, don't comment on the personality. It is actually best to avoid the phrase 'You are …' so you don't label pupils. Talk about the incident itself instead. For example, 'I saw that you punched Emily. That is totally unacceptable'.

On top of all this, remember that each lesson is a new one. Avoid reminding pupils of previous behavioural issues, in order to establish a fresh start.

16 Give pupils some support when they are working to improve their behaviour

Sometimes, pupils will need some guidance to help them improve their behaviour. You could try asking them 'What could I do to help you with this?' 'Is there any support I could be giving you to help you change this element of your behaviour?'

> ### brilliant tip
>
> Negotiate the consequences of repeated bad behaviour with the pupil. When you ask them what they think you should do if it happens again, they are often more harsh on themselves than you would have been. Then, you will come across as supportive when you let them know that you think the consequences should be less severe!

17 Make pupils aware of how they are escalating the consequences

You should be aware of your sequence of consequences. Hopefully your placement school will have a behaviour plan that everyone should follow. If you are having an issue with somebody's behaviour, make sure they are aware of where they are in that sequence of consequences, e.g.

1 Ask them to focus on their work.
2 Ask them to focus on their work or they will be moved for the lesson.
3 Move them to a different seat for the lesson.
4 Remind them to focus on their work.
5 Ask them to focus on their work or they will have to be removed to another classroom.
6 Remove them to another classroom.

Of course, before all this, you should have made sure that they weren't unfocused because they were stuck on their work. Using the sequences above, or those that the school has established, pupils cannot be surprised. It is when they are surprised that they are more likely to confront you and say 'That is so unfair!'

18 Stay calm

This is definitely a last but not least suggestion. It is very important. You have to remain calm for a number of reasons. You
cannot scare pupils or make them feel threatened, or they may
never trust you again and a pupil needs to feel secure in their
environment in order to be able to learn effectively. Secondly,
it is bad for you to get wound up. It will increase your adrena-
line levels, and possibly your blood pressure. If you overreact
in a lesson, you might feel embarrassed or ashamed about it
afterwards and you know the pupils are likely to remember it.
Lastly, angry people look ridiculous. They go red, they shout to
the point where they can't get any louder, they accidentally spit
and their bodies start to go quite rigid, like you see in comedies
(think about 'Basil' in 'Fawlty Towers'). Pupils get numbed
to angry behaviours and it will not continue to be effective in
gaining their respect, even if it did the first time. Even worse,
sometimes they can find it so funny that they will try to make it
happen in future lessons.

Discussions after class

'Stay behind.' Doesn't it make you think that you're in for a
reading of the riot act? It doesn't have to be that way. 'Stay
behind, please' can actually be turned into a beneficial experience. You can turn a negative discussion into a positive one by
asking the pupils what they think they should do differently
next time. That way, the conversation can end with you being in
agreement and saying 'Well done'.

When discussing behaviour issues, talk about them as though
they were in the past. 'Before, I noticed that you sat tapping your
pen a lot, which put me off my teaching.' It shows that you have
confidence that it is not a permanent thing. It also shows that
you are happy to forgive anything that was in the past, in order to
move on in a more positive direction. Follow it up with 'Let's ...',

so correcting their behaviour becomes a joint project between you both. Admitting to pupils that you are willing to make an effort to solve the situation often puts them at ease.

It definitely isn't advisable just to start shouting at pupils. Sometimes, it is hugely enlightening just to ask them how they are. Often, they will say 'Sorry, I'm having a bad day today' and then you can follow it up with 'So you'll be back to your normal cheerful and polite self next lesson' (establishing expectations, positive language and paying them a compliment, all in one statement). They will usually agree. If they are really grumpy, you can remind them that you like them and will be willing to forgive them by saying something like 'Usually you work really hard and are a pleasure to teach. I can see you didn't have a good day, but if your behaviour is back to normal tomorrow, it doesn't have to be a problem'. If they have never been well behaved for you, you can give them something to live up to by saying '[Class teacher's name] tells me that you had a really good start to the year. Hopefully we can continue that now so you can achieve your target level'.

brilliant tip

For any discussions with pupils that are out of the classroom or not during lesson time, it would be advisable to ask the class teacher to be there, as they will probably know the pupil better than you. To prevent false allegations being made against you, never speak to a pupil alone in a room with the door closed. If you are talking to them one-to-one, always make sure you are in view of other members of staff.

If behaviour issues continue to occur with a particular pupil, seek advice not only from the class teacher, but also from senior members of staff. They might be aware of outside factors that you don't know about and could suggest further strategies.

After all this, think about your friends at school. I am so lucky still to be friends with many of the people I went to school with. But at school, they were a nightmare! There is no way I would put up with the things that they did to their teachers at school (they were the cause of my fear of being locked in the cupboard). Yet, they are now wonderful, decent, completely trustworthy people. Even if the behaviour of some pupils is really bad, it won't necessarily be forever and they might grow up to be really likeable.

brilliant dos and don'ts

Do

- ✔ Do treat pupils with respect. They could be Nobel Prize winners in the making!
- ✔ Do act as a good role model. Part of the pupil's problem may be that they haven't already got one. You could be an excellent example to them.
- ✔ Do forgive pupils for their mistakes. We all make them and we hope that they will forgive us for any we make!
- ✔ Do know your expectations. If you expect pupils to behave fantastically, that will come across and you can work together in your aim to achieve it.
- ✔ Do use positive language. Try not to sound too negative or a nag.
- ✔ Do allow pupils some time to make the decision to follow your instruction.
- ✔ Do use humour as a tool for diffusion. It lightens the atmosphere and reminds pupils that you are human.
- ✔ Do follow through with your threatened consequences. It is very important that the pupils know exactly where they stand with you.

▶

Don't

✗   Don't belittle pupils. They may never trust you again, or even try to get their own back. To add to that, it's not fair. They have still got so much learning about behaviour to do.

✗   Don't use words that give pupils an escape route. 'Try to …' and 'If you could …' communicate that you know there's a possibility that it won't happen.

✗   Don't label the pupils e.g. aggressive. This comes back to the self-fulfilling prophecy argument above.

✗   Don't get angry – it looks ridiculous!

 **brilliant** recap

We must not be surprised when our pupils' behaviour is not perfect. They do not have the life experience that we have and unfortunately for them, they have many mistakes to make in their efforts to get it. To add to that, of course, our behaviour is not perfect either and if we make mistakes, we really appreciate being forgiven for them. It is important to make sure pupils know that we will not hold theirs against them. It is easy to become a real nag of a teacher, but when we remember that we are not just teaching the main learning objectives of the lesson, but also how to become good citizens, it highlights the importance of teaching manners and correct behaviours.

You will be right to remind pupils of acceptable behaviour and if necessary, the reasons behind it, and to provide consequences where necessary. But, make sure you always do it in a way that makes pupils feel safe and respected.

CHAPTER 14

Working with others

One of the most interesting and rewarding aspects of working as a teacher is the number of relationships you will build. It is important that you endeavour to create successful partnerships not only with your pupils, but also with other teachers, Teaching Assistants (TAs) and parents, as well as the Senior Leadership Team and other support staff. This chapter will focus on how to work successfully with teachers, TAs and parents.

Working with teachers

It is crucial that you form productive working relationships with other teachers, both in your training year and when you are employed as a qualified teacher. A teacher will respect and value you most if you:

form productive working relationships with other teachers

- are highly organised;
- show enthusiasm for delivering an effective education;
- are respectful and considerate of their priorities and obligations;
- work well as part of a team, so are prepared to share your ideas and resources, whilst valuing theirs;
- do not appear to be begrudging of expending your time and energy.

There is more information about how to work effectively with teachers in Chapter 6. It is important to be aware that it can be difficult for a teacher to let go of their pupils and pass the reins to you because they will have worked hard to build their relationship with the class.

Issues with staff

Teachers should really have excellent skills in building relationships with others, because they work closely with such a large number of people, but unfortunately this is not the case for everyone. People who work in schools are used to being in control of situations and advising people, but some can be quite odd in other situations. But then, that's true in any big organisation, isn't it? If you do happen to have any issues with a teacher, the first thing you should do is talk to your Mentor or Professional Tutor about it. They are likely to offer to have a chat with the teacher concerned, or suggest ways of dealing with them and will want to know if the situation improves. If they think it is advisable, it might be worth organising a meeting with the teacher, preferably with your Mentor present. If you are able to discuss the situation, rather than saying 'You're too …' or 'Stop being so …', try saying 'I don't know if I'm worrying too much, but I get the impression that you are not happy with my progress' (or whatever the issue is), followed by 'Is there anything I can do to improve the situation?' This sounds unaggressive and proactive. Teachers you work with may really respect the fact that you want to deal with any misunderstandings or issues, and have the confidence to talk it through.

If you have further problems with teachers, you can always rely on your Tutor from your course provider to guide you to a solution. They are likely to have come across any such issues dozens of times before.

Working with Teaching Assistants

During my training year, I wrote my dissertation on the relation-ships between Teachers and TAs, which was highly enlightening. TAs will usually be in the room for one pupil, because the funding for their time comes from an individual pupil's Statement of Educational Special Needs – a document provided to the school by the Local Education Authority (LEA) outlining the particular needs of the pupil. It contains decisions about the levels of special needs that a pupil has and what the school needs to do to provide appropriate support. For some statemented pupils, requiring a high level of assistance, the LEA will agree to fund the presence of a TA in an agreed number of lessons. However, some pupils have physical needs and the TA may be there to make sure those physical needs are met, but may then be able to help with other things in the classroom.

Sometimes, the pupil does not feel comfortable with having an adult sitting with them throughout the entire lesson, which is understandable because it makes them stand out as different. Therefore, it is a good idea for a conversation to be held between the teacher, TA and pupil, to decide that the TA will also work with others in the class, whilst ensuring the SEN pupil's needs are met.

TAs' experiences of school life vary tremendously. Sometimes, they know exactly what they are doing and some teachers give them the responsibility to make their own decisions. Some teachers are welcoming and approach the TA as soon as pos-sible in a lesson to explain what they would like the pupil to have achieved by the end of it and from which books they can gain extra information. Rarely, TAs will walk into rooms and not even raise any eye contact from the teacher. The beginning of the lesson can be the most frantic time because the teacher is ensuring pupils are settling down to their work, have the correct equipment and have finished their conversations, whilst making sure their resources are to hand and possibly preparing to take the register. Many pupils arrive with questions about homework, or something they saw on TV last night, or want to borrow something. But come on, we can at least say 'Hello'!

When I was writing my dissertation, I interviewed both teachers and TAs and found that frustration on the TA's part is frequent because quite often, they really don't know what they should be doing. Neither were they sure about how much authority they held in the classroom. They also didn't know whether to volunteer to do other tasks, such as giving out or collecting in materials. The teachers weren't sure about how much authority they should give TAs and they didn't know if they could ask TAs to do other tasks such as giving things out or collecting in materials!

discuss the TA's role
with the class teacher

It is therefore important that you discuss the TA's role with the class teacher, finding out what kinds of things they have been doing with the pupil or class so far. You also need to find out how the teacher has been communicating with the TA. For example, have they been discussing the work before or during the lessons? If you think it would be useful to use the TA in different ways, discuss it with both the class teacher and the TA before you make any decisions.

You cannot expect the TA to know exactly what you want them to do in the classroom unless the school has come up with a very good policy that everybody adheres to rigidly. My conclusions from the dissertation were that teachers and TAs need time together to plan how they will be used in the lessons and if the pupil will do any work differently from the rest of the class. In reality, that doesn't always happen. TAs don't get paid for any time except for that that they spend in the lessons. So, unfortunately, you cannot expect them to meet with you at lunchtime or after school. They are supposed to have free lessons but they are often required to do things during that time. But do find time in every lesson to tell them in what way you would like them to help and what you expect certain pupils to have achieved by the end.

brilliant tip

Some TAs find it really useful to receive a copy of the lesson plan before the lesson, giving them a chance to do some revision, or to see what they will be doing.

brilliant tip

When you give out class worksheets, it would be really useful for the TAs if you gave them a completed worksheet. Remember that they haven't received the same training as you and might not know the answers.

Try not to feel embarrassed or judged when the TA is in the lesson with you. If the pupils understand that you value the presence of the TA and appreciate their impact on education, they will feel comfortable in asking the TA for help and advice, helping the classroom to become an environment in which everybody's goal is the same – a high-quality education.

brilliant tip

If you overhear the TA trying to coerce the pupil into working, unsuccessfully, approach the pupil and let it be very clear that you agree with the TA, but also ask if there is anything you can do to make the task easier for them.

Inappropriate behaviour

Occasionally, I have witnessed behaviour from TAs that I have thought to be irresponsible, such as showing pupils family photos at inappropriate times and texting from their mobile phones. It is quite embarrassing to have to confront another adult about something you've seen or heard, but you must remember that if you allow a TA to text in a classroom, you are allowing mobile phones in your lessons.

During your training year, the best thing to do if you encounter such a situation is to discuss it with the class teacher, who ultimately has responsibility for what happens in the classroom. They might suggest that you talk to the TA. If this is the agreed course of action, ask in a friendly manner if you can quickly talk to them at the end of the lesson. Pupils will probably think that you are talking about the work. When all the pupils have left, just ask them if they could avoid doing it because you want the pupils to know that we respect the rules as much as we want them to.

Having said all of that, such events are extremely rare. It is wonderful to have the assistance of TAs. They are often really encouraging and say supportive things about an activity you have set, boosting your morale. They often mention if they think something hasn't been understood clearly, which is very useful. It is also great to have another adult in the room sometimes (someone who wants the lesson to go as well as you do). That is without even mentioning the fact that by being there, they are helping to make your lesson accessible to all pupils. They reduce frustration for some pupils and make their lives much easier, as well as increasing their chance of reaching their potential.

Working with parents

The importance of creating a positive relationship with parents cannot be underestimated. They are a huge influence on your pupils' lives and their support is incredibly effective. There are a number of times in which you will work with parents, including parents' evenings, sending letters of praise and contacting them when you need further support.

Your communication should always be focused around the progress the pupil is or isn't making. That is what the parent will usually be most interested in and what they want you to be concentrating on. Make it very clear from the outset that if the communication is about a concern that you have, you are working to find a solution, to ensure that their child can make good progress in your lessons. Even if you have been upset by a pupil, it is important that you don't let your emotions get in the way.

> your communication should always be focused around the progress the pupil is or isn't making

brilliant tip

Before you decide to communicate with parents, speak to the class teacher and possibly your Mentor. Some schools have policies about how you should do this and how you should report it afterwards. The teachers might also be familiar with the parents, so could offer specific advice.

Phoning home

Behavioural issues

It is tempting, when you have had a difficult experience with a pupil, to phone home and moan about them, hoping the parent will step in and give them a few ultimatums about working at school and the treats or punishment they will receive at home. However, this could easily get the parents off side. We have to remember that, in a way, children are an extension of their parents and if we insult their child, or make them out to sound bad, we could make the parents feel that they have to defend them.

Think about what you are hoping to achieve in this phone call. It shouldn't be to get it off your chest – there are other members of staff and trainees you can do this to. If you are phoning to try to improve the pupil's behaviour, you should stick to facts rather than emotions when talking to parents.

brilliant tip

When describing something, one way to prevent what you say from raising emotions is to avoid the use of adjectives. 'Danny broke a ruler' is less likely to sound aggressive than 'Danny was behaving stupidly'.

One productive use of a phone call home is to find out if there is anything going on, especially if a behavioural issue you would like to talk about is unusual. For example, you could say 'Sarah has not been herself in the last few weeks and has seemed less focused than usual. Have you noticed anything similar at home?' This is better than directly asking parents to reveal personal issues. Often, you'll find out that something is happening, such as a close relative being ill. Then, you can use this to have a chat with the pupil at a discreet moment and let them know that you are aware that they have other things on their mind and you understand why their behaviour is different, to be able to use this as a basis to discuss strategies to deal with it. For example, you could provide them with a 'time out to another room' pass if needed.

If the conversation reveals no explanation for the behaviour, you could ask the parent to talk to the pupil about the importance of good behaviour, or again, more constructively, you could ask if they could recommend strategies for dealing with it, considering the fact that they know the pupil better than you do. This is, of course, after you have told them that you have used all your usual strategies and you are at the point where you will have to take more serious action.

If it is clear to the parent that you are using this conversation to move forward in a positive direction, they are likely to be supportive. Sometimes, parents will mistake a phone call home for the teacher not taking their own action and relying too soon on further help.

If, a few months down the line, the behaviour has continued to expose itself, you could phone again and say that what they did last time was effective for a while, would they mind doing it again? Of course, this demonstrates how useful it can be to phone parents who have had a successful input to the child's behaviour. When you thank them and say something positive about their child, they will know you don't only look for the bad things.

Behaviour contracts

If the bad behaviour persists, it is important to ask parents to come in to school, after discussing it with the class teacher, again for a positive experience. It is useful when parents come in to say that we are having a few difficulties in class because of … (mention behaviours, not personality traits) and we are here to try to find a way to increase … (mention a good behaviour that you are looking for). Appendix 3 is an example of a behaviour contract I use, adapted from Rogers (1998). It contains an admittance of the behaviour that needs to be changed, plus how you intend to work together to change it.

brilliant tip

If you would like to meet with parents, make sure the class teacher is also there. Be prepared for the fact that you might have to explain that you are a trainee.

It is important to let the pupil know at this stage that you are on their side. Allow them a chance during the meeting to have their say. It might be that they pick up on an aspect of you or your teaching that they don't like. Don't be offended by this. Firstly, it can be difficult for a pupil to have a parent feeling angry with them, so it is natural for them to want to shift the blame. Secondly, if you allow yourself to get dragged into an argument with them, you are diminishing your authoritative role. Just say 'OK …' and then either explain why you need to do these things or even tell them that you'll bear in mind that they get annoyed when you do that. That does not take any authority away from you. It shows that you respect them enough to listen to what they have to say and that makes it easier for them to respect you back.

Sometimes, a pupil will make a valid point about something you have done, or a way they have felt in your lesson. It is perfectly acceptable, if you can see their point, to let them know that you can understand and even apologise if you think it appropriate. Classrooms are such busy places and sometimes you might say things that come out the wrong way or even phrase an instruction badly, while you have seven other pupils standing next to you, all expecting your attention. If you apologise to the pupil, it just shows them that you respect their opinion. The parent really shouldn't judge you for that.

brilliant tip

Owing to the hustle and bustle of the classroom, it can be difficult to remember word-for-word what you have said or what a pupil has said. This makes it very embarrassing if a parent or pupil quotes you on something that you can't remember saying, or if you are asked what the pupil did or said. It is therefore useful to have a notebook nearby to write down exactly what happened, before you are distracted by something else.

Allow the pupil to suggest ways in which you can both deal with their behaviour. They know themselves better than you, after all. If they think they should sit somewhere else, let them choose where, stressing the objective of less disruptive behaviour. Also have a section in your behaviour plan to say what you can do to support them with this change and stick to it.

At the end of the report, establish a reward system, both at school and at home (it might be wise to discuss this with the parent beforehand). That will ensure you remain in contact with people at home and will give the pupil something to work towards. If the parent agrees, allow the pupil to have an input into what that reward will be, to embed the teamwork aspect of the meeting.

brilliant example

I worked with one pupil whom I had started to think less and less of. I held a meeting with his mum and we had a good, positive discussion, so it was clear that this meeting was about making progress. When we asked him to think of a reward from home that he would really work towards, he said he would like to spend the day fishing with his uncle. How can you dislike someone who chooses that over any other treat? It's amazing what you learn about pupils when you get the chance.

The pupil's attitude towards learning

Sometimes, a pupil will not mess around and will be respectful of your rules, but you may still have concerns about the fact that they don't seem bothered about whether or not they meet the learning objectives. This is as much of an issue as anything behavioural. Communication with parents can be very valuable here. You could find out from talking to parents what the pupil is interested in, in order to be able to relate their learning to it. Nonchalance can arise from pupils not knowing what they want to do with their life, for example, or maybe from fear of failing their National Curriculum Assessments. It can be beneficial again to talk to a parent about this, to discuss how you can both help.

Parents' evenings

Parents' evenings too can be very positive occasions. You will find that the class teacher will do the majority of the talking, but will introduce you and either they or the parents might ask for your input. Don't be dreamy and say everything is fine when it isn't, but do turn any nagging into striving for development. It is important to talk about progress made (or not) and other factual information. It is also useful to make sure they have no further questions. Remember, the pupil may have, at home, blamed a lack of progress on you. Don't be offended by that, but calmly put the case right. On the other hand, it is wonderful to have the opportunity to say really nice things about pupils who deserve it.

Angry parents

Sometimes, it might seem that a parent has come to a parents' evening expecting an argument, if they are not happy about something. There is a branch of Science, called Neuro-linguistic Programming (NLP), that would say, in this situation, you can build up a rapport with the parent, making them less aggressive towards you, by speaking at the same speed as them and slightly matching their body language. Obviously, don't match their body language completely. They'll think you're taking the mickey! But if they lean slightly to their right, you could lean slightly to your right, but in a different position. If they lean forward, you could lean forward a bit too. On a more sophisticated level, you could listen out for their use of language to detect if they are a visual, auditory or kinaesthetic learner (see Chapter 7) and start to incorporate that kind of language into what you say. For example, 'I see what you mean', 'I hear what you're saying' or 'It seems to me that …'. I'm not sure; that feels a little bit manipulative to me. But there are some strong believers in it, so by all means try it.

One other recommendable way of dealing with this situation would be to open up your body language into a non-threatening position (arms down on your lap, not leaning towards them, head to one side to show that you are listening) and speak slowly, clearly and calmly. It is then difficult for them to remain agitated and you will have a more productive conversation.

brilliant tip

One last thing to remember when contacting parents is to contact the right one. Pupils often have parents living in different houses and there is usually one main contact, who doesn't necessarily share what you have said with the other. Your school will have details of both for emergency reasons, but will have a system for showing you which the priority contact is. If you phone the wrong one, you may be causing all sorts of arguments between the parents about who is looking after the pupil better.

Communicating the positive

As a trainee teacher, you will have a busy workload and it is easy to forget to recognise positive things, such as gratitude for the help a teacher has given you, acknowledgement of something you have seen them do that you thought worked really well, the fact that the TA's work has made the lesson run smoothly and accessible to all, or the fact that a pupil has achieved a particularly high grade in a test and you would like the parents to know. It's really important to make time for this kind of communication.

brilliant dos and don'ts

Do

✔ Do keep your language positive, whoever you are working with, always keeping it focused on what you are trying to achieve.

✔ Do talk about behaviours, rather than personalities, when working with anybody. There will never be a need to make it personal.

✔ Do stay professional when dealing with parents. At a parents' evening, the first thing you should talk about is progress, not behaviour.

✔ Do make the effort to make positive comments to all of these people whenever possible. That way, if ever you are concerned about something, it won't feel like you are only willing to contact people when there are problems.

Don't

✘ Don't just moan, either to a teacher, Teaching Assistant or parent. Always make sure it's clear that you want to find a solution.

✘ Don't be afraid to seek advice on any of these matters from your Mentor or Professional Tutor.

brilliant recap

It is hard to think of a job in which you'd be required to form relationships with so many different people. It's one of the most challenging and rewarding aspects of the job. It is therefore crucial to build relationships that are positive and centred around learning.

It is important when communicating with teachers, TAs and parents to keep the progress of pupils as a focus. This is what you are all working together to achieve. Sometimes, working with so many people can result in situations that evoke emotional behaviour. If you experience this from others, remain empathetic, as there will often be reasons for it, sometimes about issues that are deeper than you are aware of. Always make sure the people you are working with know that all you want from this communication is for your pupils to learn as well as they can. If you are feeling emotional yourself, take some time out before you talk to any of the people involved.

Also, remember to communicate the positive things. This will make sure people understand that you are fair and friendly.

PART 5

Looking ahead

CHAPTER 15

Applying for jobs

When to do it

So, you've enjoyed your training year and are ready to embark upon your career as a Qualified Teacher. It is advisable that you start applying for jobs as early as the January or February of your training year. This might seem

> start applying for jobs as early as the January or February of your training year

premature, but well-organised schools, or those that know they are about to have a vacancy due to retirement, for example, will want to advertise early, because they will have more of an opportunity to recruit from a wide range of candidates. People already in teaching jobs are required to provide at least half a term's notice to be able to enter another teaching job, so they will be looking at around this time. Schools advertising jobs from June onwards will therefore know that the applications they receive will not be from currently working teachers, but from people in their training year or those returning to teaching. So, lesser experienced teachers may feel they have more of a chance to stand out at this later time of year, but some people prefer to have their job decided to enable them to make necessary arrangements, such as accommodation.

How to find jobs

There are a huge number of ways to find teaching jobs. If you know the area in which you wish to teach, you should go to that

LEA's website, which might allow you to input some information in order to receive automatic job alerts. There is also the Schools Recruitment Service (see web address in Appendix 4), but many people choose to visit the specialised teaching job websites, such as the TES website, on which you can type in your chosen area and Key Stage, in order for it to bring up only the jobs relevant to you. The 'teachernet' website contains an up-to-date and highly comprehensive list of links to websites available for this. Lastly, many schools also advertise their jobs in the local newspapers.

brilliant tip

If there is a school that you know you would particularly like to work for, it might be worth writing to them with a letter to say why you would like to work for that school (more information about this later in the chapter), enclose your CV and ask them to keep it on file in case any jobs become available. Make it clear in your letter that you would be happy to meet them if they would like to discuss it further.

Your application

Many schools will ask for you to send in a letter of application and your CV to apply for the job.

Letter of application

Before you write your letter of application, take a look at the school's website. Even better, ask to visit the school in advance. They really won't mind this. Or, if you know of anybody that already works in that school, talk to them. What you really need to find out is a list of the school's current priorities. For example, it

find out the school's current priorities

might be modernising learning using e-learning, assessment for learning, pupil voice (using pupils as part of a team for the development of school life) or it might be meeting individual needs. If you can relate anything you have done or any interests that you have to their priority areas, your application will stand out.

brilliant tip

It is also wise, if they have written one, to read carefully the 'person specification' – the section that lists the attributes the school is looking for in the candidates. You would need to make sure you demonstrate that they apply to you in either your letter of application, CV or application form (see below).

Ofsted reports

Make sure you read the most recent Ofsted report for the school (the web address is in Appendix 4), which will highlight areas of strength that you might become involved in, and areas for development. If you have particular skills that could help the school in working on this development, make sure you mention these somewhere in the application.

You will need to write why you are applying for this particular job, to make sure it doesn't look as though you are just applying for every similar job in the area. Also write about why you think you would be an ideal candidate for this job.

Here follows an example of a letter of application:

brilliant example

Dear [name of Headteacher, or other name if made specific on the job details]

▶

I am writing to apply for the post of Early Years Class Teacher [*use the exact words as stated in the job details*]. I am currently in my training year and by July, I will have worked with Early Years and Key Stages 1 and 2, but I would very much like to teach Early Years, specialising in numeracy.

I am applying for this post because I would like to become involved in your work on meeting individual needs. I hold a particular interest in this area as my research project during my training year was on engaging pupils with particular learning needs. As you will see in my CV, I also have some experience in working with groups of pupils with Special Educational Needs. Other skills I have to offer your school include a competent use of technology and e-learning, good organisation and an ability to build positive relationships with pupils.

Please find enclosed my CV. If you would like to discuss this application further, please do not hesitate to contact me using the details above [*you will have given your telephone numbers, address and e-mail address*]. I look forward to hearing from you.

Yours sincerely,

Signature

[Name]

Enclosure: CV

Your CV

Your CV should have your contact details at the top, followed by a personal statement, which is a paragraph that gives the reader an idea about who you are as a teacher. For example:

'I am an organised, hard-working and conscientious teacher, specialising in numeracy. My teaching style is interactive, incorporating activities that are visual, auditory and kinaesthetic in every lesson. I also integrate ICT into my lessons as much as possible, with regular use of individual computers, animations, and assessment programs and websites. I have a strong interest in meeting individual needs and also in healthy schools. In my current placement school, I have been running a healthy-cooking club. I have a passion for delivering high-quality, stimulating education.'

You will then need to list your teaching experience, outlining the Key Stages with which you have worked and any subject specialism. Following that, you will need to list your education, including grades. Next, you should list your previous jobs, mentioning the skills you developed in these roles. If you have too many to fit into the recommended two A4 sides, just list the jobs most relevant to teaching and the specialist knowledge that you have.

Then, include a section about your additional skills, such as languages you speak, computer programs you are able to use and if you are able to drive a minibus. After that, the school will want to know a bit about you as a person, so include a section about your interests and achievements; things that you do in your spare time and other qualifications, such as sport coaching and any awards you have won. Lastly, write the names and contact details of two referees, one from a placement school and one from your course tutor.

brilliant tip

Ask your course tutor or your Professional Tutor if they would mind reading your letter of application and CV, to see if they have any suggestions.

Application forms

Some schools have an application form which contains questions, I guess depending on what they're most interested in. It is very important here to come across as professional and to highlight your organisation and positive attitude towards the pupils. At some point, if appropriate, include something to let them know that your classroom management style is calm and positive. Also make sure they know that you enjoy working using modern teaching methods, as one of the things they love about new teachers is the fact that they are adaptable. In fact, try to include your enthusiasm to use as many aspects of teaching as possible from Chapters 7–10.

brilliant tip

Many LEAs will have a template application form that the school will use, which means that you can save one as a master, in order to save you time if you have to apply for a few more in that area. However, you must always adapt it to the priorities and achievements of the school in question.

If you get called in for an interview

Congratulations! The following part of the chapter will let you know what you can expect from the interview day.

You will be written to with an agenda for your day, starting with the time of arrival. If it's at all possible, try to find the school before the day, because a school can be such a big place that even if you find it on the map, you can spend ten minutes working your way around the perimeter to find the entrance. Remember also that it will take longer getting to a school at the beginning of the day when lots of buses and parents will be driving in the surrounding area. When you arrive, go straight to the reception and explain that you are there for the interview and let them know the name of the person on the letter of invitation. Put aside the whole day for your interview. Although it might be inconvenient, it would not look good if halfway through a conversation, you tell the interviewers that you have to catch your train at four o'clock. Some interviews will go on until six o'clock, depending on the number of applicants and some will finish at half past two, but it's wise to give the impression that this interview is the most important thing on your mind.

It is likely that your day will start with a tour of the school, probably by a member of the Senior Leadership Team, who will be trying to gain information about what kind of teacher you are from the very start. It's a good idea to acknowledge things that impress you and to ask any appropriate questions that come to mind. You will come across as being switched on and interested in doing a good job, rather than being somebody who just wants any job they can get.

At some point during the day, you will be expected to teach at least part of a lesson. The school will have included in their letter of invitation what that lesson should be about. The tips in Chapter 12 about how to structure your lesson so you don't forget anything and the importance of taking risks with exciting activities, rather than sticking to safe bookwork, will suit this situation well.

brilliant tip

Telephone the school before the interview and ask if there will be any pupils in the class you will be teaching with individual learning needs. For example, do any resources need to be enlarged or is there anybody who will not be able to move easily around the classroom? This is crucial information for delivering a successful lesson, but also shows that you are thinking carefully about the impact of it on all pupils.

Prepare your lesson well and make any resources, such as sorting cards or templates, yourself. If you laminate cards in advance,

prepare your lesson well and make any resources yourself

it will demonstrate that you didn't leave the planning to the last minute. Don't take it for granted that the classroom will have ICT equipment. If you require an overhead projector, telephone the school to make sure they have one available. You could also ask which interactive projection program they use (if they use one), for example 'Interwrite' or 'SMART', so you can make sure that you are familiar with it. Then, put your necessary files onto a memory stick because it might be easier for them if you use a computer that is already connected to the projector, rather than your own laptop.

brilliant tip

Take two copies of your lesson plan for this lesson or section of lesson, one for you and one to give the observer. Also take some good examples from previous lessons, so they know you don't just plan well for interviews.

Pupil interviews

The ethos of using 'pupil voice' is becoming more of a priority in schools now. This means that pupils are able to discuss with certain members of staff the quality of their education, including which methods of teaching they feel they learn the most from. They also contribute towards discussions about the way the school is run. For this reason, especially at the secondary level, it is quite likely that you will be asked to have a conversation with some pupils, possibly without another member of staff there. The pupils might view this as a bit of an interview themselves and ask you lots of questions, or you might be required to start the conversation yourself.

Pupils are surprisingly perceptive about what makes a good teacher and will not want you to behave like a friend. They, just like the Headteacher, will be looking for somebody who behaves professionally and who comes across as knowing what they are doing and caring about the education they deliver. It would be wise here to bring into the conversation the importance of varying the activities and making sure they are interactive, as pupils do not generally enjoy lessons when the teacher either talks all the time, or hands out worksheet after worksheet.

The interview

You will of course be asked to an interview, which is likely to include a panel of the Headteacher, your potential line manager (such as Head of Department or Key Stage) and a Governor, and is likely to last for about half an hour. They will be hoping to employ somebody who is:

● interested in their particular school;

● able to cope under stressful situations;

● open to new ideas in teaching;

● enthusiastic;

● calm and focused, including in their behaviour management style;

● up to date with the latest ideas in teaching (see page 22);

● organised;

● skilled in ICT;

● able to demonstrate their good subject/specialism knowledge.

brilliant tip

Read a few editions of the *Times Educational Supplement* and relevant teaching magazines in advance, to be up to date with what is happening in teaching. They should be available in the library of your training institution.

So, try to demonstrate or talk about all of the above things during your interview. The kinds of questions they may ask include:

- 'How do you think your lesson went (*referring to the one you taught that day*)?'
- 'Tell us about a successful lesson you have taught and what made it successful.'
- 'Tell us about a less successful lesson and what you have learned from it.'
- 'Describe the action you would take to stop low-level disruption (e.g. talking over you or fidgeting).'
- 'What skills do you have to offer the rest of your team?'
- 'What could other teachers learn from you?'
- 'Tell us about your interests and hobbies and how they influence your teaching.'
- 'Give an example of a recent time when you have made a mistake and what you did about it.'
- 'How would you incorporate Af L into your lessons?'
- 'Why do you think that assessing and recording students' marks are so important?'
- 'If one of your pupils wasn't achieving their target level in your lesson, how would you push them to get there?'
- 'How do you differentiate in your lessons?'
- 'Given the students' levels in each class, how would you know what material to teach for these classes?'
- 'How would you motivate students that are not self-motivated?'
- 'How would you help with extra-curricular activities in this school?'
- 'One of your Gifted and Talented students is causing disruption in your lessons. How would you deal with this?'

- 'What other methods would you use to engage your Gifted and Talented pupils?'

- 'If you were to get this job, where do you see yourself in 5 years?'

- 'A young girl comes up to you and asks if she can talk to you in confidence. How would you respond to this and what would you do?'

brilliant tip

Some people are quite hard in interviews and might be speaking to you in a way that doesn't appear to be very encouraging. They might be a bit 'old school' – testing your nerve! Remain calm and accurate in what you say, to show that you can cope with it. You can be sure they've done it to everybody else too.

brilliant tip

Sit with both feet on the ground and your hands on your lap. Try not to fold your arms as it makes you look a bit defensive. If you're a fidgeter, hold your hands together.

What to wear

You might be concerned about overdressing for the occasion and looking too keen, but you will not look out of place if you wear a suit and if you're male, a shirt done up to the top and a tie, or if you're female, a smart top underneath, with a neckline not far below the base of your neck. It is a good idea to wear flat shoes, as you might be taken for a tour of the school grounds.

If it's going really well …

I only recommend this if you're feeling quite confident that you might get the job. For example, if the school asked you to apply and if you know that you are the only candidate (it can happen), it would be worth asking if you could commence employment as soon as your course ends, for example on 1 July. That might involve you being used to cover lessons for absent teachers in July, which is far from ideal, but it would mean that you would be paid over the summer.

brilliant dos and don'ts

Do

✔ Do tactfully show off all your skills. Rather than worrying about sounding arrogant, try to make yourself stand out.

✔ Do remain professional throughout, even if you are with teachers and other employees who aren't on your interview panel. Word does get around.

✔ Do feel free to speak to the pupils as you are shown into lessons, as long as they aren't meant to be silent. The staff there will be pleased to see that you are easily able to build a rapport with them.

✔ Do take some lunch, just in case they don't provide it!

✔ Do stay for the whole day, even if something at the beginning of the day puts you off. You will gain valuable experience and you might find out more information later in the day that makes you feel better.

✔ Do persevere. People often have to apply for many jobs before they are offered one. See the applications and interviews as experience. You will get quicker at writing the applications!

Don't

✘ Don't feel like you can't talk to the other candidates. A relaxed atmosphere will help you to enjoy your day. It will also show that you are able to work with others.

✘ Don't feel that you have to accept the job if at the end of the day you really don't want it. However, do give a valid reason if you don't accept.

brilliant recap

Applying for jobs can be quite stressful and there might be times when you feel you are reeling off applications one after the other. However, to make yourself stand out, it is important to find out what the school are looking for either by visiting, asking other people or by reading the most recent Ofsted report. Then, show them that you have the skills they need.

Prepare well for your interview. If possible, get somebody to help you practise answering questions, including those in this chapter. Also prepare your sample lesson thoroughly, even going into the detail of finding out if there are any pupils in the class for whom you should take special measures. The better prepared you are, the more relaxed you will feel. Remember that your interaction with the pupils will also be judged, even by the pupils themselves, so try to put your nerves aside, remain positive, professional, and show them that you have confidence in your own ability.

CHAPTER 16

Preparing for
your first job

Now you have your first job, you will want to create a strong first impression to the staff and pupils and make the change to your own life as easy as possible.

visit the school for a day at the end of the preceding summer term

Yet, the beginning of term might seem a bit daunting. One of the best things you can do to prepare yourself for this new step is to visit the school for a day at the end of the preceding summer term. Your school will probably ask you to do so anyway, but if they don't, give them a call to ask if there would be a suitable day for you to go in. They are unlikely to see this as hassle, but will probably be glad that you are keen to organise yourself as well as possible.

Things to take when you visit your school

- A notebook that will be kept handy throughout the day to make notes of anything, such as times, pass codes and the names of members of staff you meet.

- A memory stick, for you to be able to take electronic copies of important files.

- A laptop if you would like to be able to put those files straight onto your computer.

- Lunch, in case they don't provide it.

People to try to meet during your visit

- The Head of the Year of your teaching group or tutor group (some schools have similar roles entitled 'Learning Mentors'). This will help you know who to go to if you encounter any pastoral issues in your first few days. They might also be able to share with you their priorities for that group of pupils.

- Resource and equipment technicians. Find out from them how much notice they require to be able to either prepare equipment or make resources. They will be pleased that you do not intend to give them things to do at the last minute.

- Your Head of Department (may be called the Subject Leader) or Head of Key Stage, if applicable, although you will probably have met them on your interview day.

- Fellow teachers. It would be nice to see some familiar faces on your first day.

Things to take home from the school

Ask for the following, if they are available:

- your timetable;

- class lists, together with information about any SEN pupils you might have in the class;

- a list of the topics you will be teaching at the beginning of term, plus any schemes of work;

- policy documents, for example, rewards and sanctions, punctuality, 'Every Child Matters' and 'Meeting Individual Needs' policies, plus any general staff policies;

- a list of term dates and training days. Don't rely on the LEA website for term dates, as schools have a small element of flexibility in their own dates. Make sure you know if your first day or days in September are teaching days or training days. You need this information for your planning.

> ### ☼ brilliant tip
>
> In order to familiarise yourself with what the students will need to learn, ask to borrow one of each relevant textbook, to use at home when you are lesson planning.

> ### ☼ brilliant tip
>
> To be able to plan accurately, you will need to know what equipment and resources you will have constant access to. Ask if you will have the use of a laptop and projector and find out which textbooks pupils will be able to use. If you will be teaching practical lessons, such as Art, Design, Science or PE, make sure you know which things you have to order and which things will be in your teaching room.

Over the summer

Most importantly, it's been a challenging year, so try to take the time to relax and build up your energy reserves. However, if you also spend some time planning your lessons, for

> take the time to relax and build up your energy reserves

at least the first couple of weeks of the new term, you will make the start to your new job much smoother. It takes a surprising amount of energy in the first few weeks of a teaching job to learn the names of the pupils and staff, to find your way around and to get to grips with the systems and routines. You will also need to give priority to building productive relationships with your pupils, even if that means spending time with them in detention, to make sure they know you will not be a walkover!

It can be useful to spend a few lessons with your new classes establishing ground rules. This doesn't mean you lecture them for the whole lesson, but that you take the time to explain fully your expectations at every stage. For example, if you were planning an Art lesson, you might decide to deliver a simple, short activity, but plan to spend time explaining exactly how pupils should pack away. Should there be sink monitors? Should certain pupils use a particular sink? You will then give pupils time to meet those expectations, but if they do not conduct themselves as expected, you might ask the pupils to sit down, in order to be able to explain the rules again. A Science teacher might explain to their class that the first three lessons will be about ensuring pupils are safe during practical work and ask them to do some standard practical activities, to allow the teacher to observe closely. Of course, rewards should be used when pupils meet your expectations. If you spend your time establishing routines and expectations now, it will make the rest of your year much easier.

You will probably have been given schemes of work, or at least a list of the topics you will be teaching. If you spend a decent amount of time planning these lessons before the start of term, you will give the impression to your pupils of being organised and efficient, which will earn you some respect immediately. If you also take into account the SEN requirements of particular pupils in your classes, you will make them feel that they are in safe hands.

brilliant tip

Although you might feel tired after your training year, if you can, do your lesson planning before the end of the summer term. That way, you will be able to ensure that you have the resources that you are hoping for. You certainly can't expect the technicians to prepare it all on the first day back.

If you have time, read through all of the policy documents you are given. You will then know what to expect and use the correct procedures with your pupils, which will dampen any ideas that you don't know what you're doing.

 **tip**

Don't assume that you will be able to telephone the school for further information during the holidays. You might find that there is nobody there to answer the call.

brilliant dos and don'ts

Do

✔ Do expect to spend the whole day there and make the most of meeting people and gaining valuable information.

✔ Do, if you are concerned, ask for the e-mail address of your line manager (e.g. Head of Subject or Key Stage) and ask politely if you might e-mail them if any questions come to mind.

✔ Do ask questions if there is anything you're not sure of.
For example, if the schemes of work contain only the basic objectives of the lessons, but with no suggestions for activities, ask if there is a way they would recommend of getting lesson ideas. Teachers might tell you about a good website that they use.

✔ Do try to relax during the holiday. September and October can be the most energy-consuming months of the year, even for an experienced teacher.

Don't

✘ Don't feel that you would be imposing or expecting too much to visit the school in the summer term. It is standard practice.

✘ Don't expect to get paid to visit the school before the start of your contract.

 recap

There is a lot of information that, if you gather it in advance, will make the start to your new job run smoothly, because in your first few days, the most important things to concentrate on are your routines and your relationships with pupils. Rather than collecting this information by phone or e-mail, you will gain a better understanding of procedures if you actually visit the school and meet the people with whom you will be working.

Try to gain all the information you will need to be able to plan your first couple of weeks' lessons in detail, so you can start your job feeling prepared and confident, something that the pupils will perceive and respect you for.

Conclusion: Staying sane

Teaching does not deserve the bad press it sometimes receives. It doesn't have to take over your life. If you allow it to do so, you're endangering yourself of becoming resentful of it, which makes you grumpy in the classroom and the pupils don't respond well to that! The aim of *Brilliant Trainee Teacher* is to provide you with ideas and strategies to help you become a successful teacher and to help you save time and energy by establishing positive working relationships and an effective learning environment from the outset.

There is no limit to the amount of time you can spend on teaching well, including the planning, preparation and assessment. Here are a few tips to help you maintain a work–life balance and therefore enjoy teaching as a career, not a lifestyle:

- Learn to prioritise. Maybe use Microsoft Outlook, or iCal, for example, with the due date facility, so you can plan what tasks you will complete on which days. That way, you shouldn't feel overwhelmed by them all buzzing around inside your head at the same time.

- Know what's important. At the end of the day, if you didn't get round to marking your books on the evening you were hoping to, there's no point in lying awake worrying about it. Otherwise, you'll be too tired to do it the next day. I'm not saying books don't have to be marked. But if you're a day later than you hoped in doing it, no one is going to be harmed because of it. However, if you are worried about a pupil's safety, it is worth dropping all other plans to make sure that you have discussed it with the right people.

- Keep your hobbies. This will act as a reminder of why you are working so hard in the first place – to give you a stable income to help you enjoy your life.

- Keep to a routine. If some of your hobbies take place at a certain time each week, it will mean that there is no decision to be made on those evenings about whether or not you should stay in and do some more work. However, your hobbies, if they involve an instructor, do need to be taught by people who understand that you cannot miss parents' evenings and other compulsory events.

- You might have to do some work at weekends, but I strongly advise that you keep at least a day a week free to allow you to do the things you enjoy. It will help you to return to work on Monday feeling refreshed and that you made the most of your time off.

- To maintain as much free time as possible, it is crucial to be efficient at work. I find that I don't waste a minute. Also, I walk quite fast! I also recommend working on your typing skills when you can. The ability to type fast and to use basic computer programs will save you lots of time when lesson planning, making resources, writing reports, responding to e-mails, sharing ideas, inputting data – everything.

- It might be wise to set yourself rules, such as not working past 9 o'clock at night. It is imperative that you have some switch-off time, or you're in danger of lying in bed thinking about what you've just been doing.

- Keep fit and healthy, by eating and sleeping well and doing plenty of exercise. I really believe that this helps with focus and energy levels.

- Don't forget the people around you. The trainee teaching year can seem very absorbing and will require the support of friends and family. Don't be afraid to ask them for help on taking your mind off things, or even to prepare resources. Also remember to ask them how their day was.

- Don't take bad behaviour personally. Even if a pupil is rude to you, it is likely to be a purely reactive, possibly irrational response, even if it doesn't seem like it at the time. Young people go through this and will hopefully learn from these situations.

- If at any time you feel that you just have too much to do and you are feeling seriously stressed, talk to your Mentor, either from your training institution or from your school. They might be able to help you prioritise and if they are concerned about you, they might even be able to take certain tasks off your hands, especially if they think it's a one-off.

- If all else fails, plan an adventure or some relaxation time in your holidays. When you remind yourself that you have a few weeks to play with, it all seems worth it!

My last piece of advice, to help you maintain peace of mind, is to join a Union. Unions offer help and advice and are always trying to make sure that teachers' pay and conditions are kept at a good standard. They also offer legal help if a situation arises in your work that requires it.

Finally, good luck and stick with it! Teaching is a challenging job and one that is highly rewarding in both security and satisfaction. I hope you enjoy your pupils' achievements and laughter as much as I have so far.

Appendices

Appendix 1
Teacher training courses

Please note: the following information comes from the Training and Development Agency website (http:// www. tda.gov.uk). Please consult this website for the most up-to-date information.

Type of ITT course	Qualifications required	Length of course (based on full-time study)	When to apply	How to apply	Other comments
Undergraduate Teacher Training (BEd)	• A GCSE grade C or above (or equivalent) in Mathematics and English; • A GCSE grade C or above in Science if teaching at the primary level or secondary level; • 2 A-levels (or equivalent).	3–4 years, but maybe shorter if you have other undergraduate credits.	Between September and January of the year before you wish to start.	Through UCAS.	This course allows the successful applicant to achieve QTS, whilst covering everything that a teacher at their chosen Key Stage will need to know.

Type of ITT course	Qualifications required	Length of course (based on full-time study)	When to apply	How to apply	Other comments
BA/BSc with QTS	• A GCSE grade C or above (or equivalent) in Mathematics and English; • A GCSE grade C or above in Science if teaching at the primary level or secondary level; • 2 A-levels (or equivalent).	3–4 years.	Between September and January of the year before you wish to start.	Through UCAS.	This course differs from the BEd in that the successful student gains an honours degree in a subject of their choice, whilst also being awarded QTS.
Post Graduate Certificate in Education (PGCE)	• A GCSE grade C or above (or equivalent) in Mathematics and English; • A GCSE grade C or above in Science if teaching at the primary level or secondary level; • A degree at a pass level.	1 year, if your subject ties directly in with a teaching subject. If your degree subject is unrelated, you may have to undertake further training to be able to teach a National Curriculum subject.	Between September and June of the year before you wish to start. However, it is advisable to apply earlier than June, to avoid your application being part of the last-minute rush.	Through the Graduate Teacher Training Registry (GTTR), but it is worth contacting the chosen University or College, because some require people to apply to them directly.	The PGCE is usually a mixture of time in University or College and time in school. However, it may be completed by a SCITT (school-centred initial teacher training) programme where the student is in the school full-time.

Type of ITT course	Qualifications required	Length of course (based on full-time study)	When to apply	How to apply	Other comments
School-centred Initial Teacher Training (SCITT)	• A GCSE grade C or above (or equivalent) in Mathematics and English; • A GCSE grade C or above in Science if teaching at the primary level or secondary level; • A degree at a pass level.	1 year (usually September–June), if your subject ties directly in with a teaching subject. If your degree subject is unrelated, you may have to undertake further training to be able to teach a National Curriculum subject.	During the preceding academic year; earlier rather than later is recommended.	Through the Graduate Teacher Training Registry, but it is worth contacting the chosen University or College (see the TDA website), because some require people to apply to them directly.	This course is more school-centred than the PGCE. Students will join the schools earlier in the course and conduct the vast majority of their training within the schools.
Graduate Teacher Programme (GTP)	• A GCSE grade C or above (or equivalent) in Mathematics and English; • A GCSE grade C or above in Science if teaching at the primary level or secondary level; • A degree at a pass level.	1 year, if your subject ties directly in with a teaching subject. If your degree subject is unrelated, you may have to undertake further training to be able to teach a National Curriculum subject.	When you find an appropriate post.	Find a school willing to employ you on this basis. Then apply via your local Employment Based Initial Teacher Training (EBITT) provider. For further details and to find such schools, consult the Training and Development Agency for Schools (TDA).	Experience in teaching or a related discipline is required. Although individuals may qualify for a financial incentive on the other courses, this course provides a higher salary.

Type of ITT course	Qualifications required	Length of course (based on full-time study)	When to apply	How to apply	Other comments
Registered Teacher Programme (RTP)	• A GCSE grade C or above (or equivalent) in Mathematics and English; • A GCSE grade C or above in Science if teaching at the primary level or secondary level; • The equivalent of 2 years higher education training or qualification (240 CATS points).	Up to 2 years, depending on whether you have any teaching experience.	At any time.	Find a school willing to employ you on this basis. Let them know that they may be able to receive funding from the Government. Then apply via your local Employment Based Initial Teacher Training (EBITT) provider. For further details, consult the TDA.	Although individuals may qualify for a financial incentive on the other courses, this course provides a higher salary. This course is not available in Wales.

Type of ITT course	Qualifications required	Length of course (based on full-time study)	When to apply	How to apply	Other comments
Teach First	• A 2:1 degree or above (40% of which needs to tie in with a National Curriculum subject); • An A-level at grade B or above, in a subject that ties in with the National Curriculum; • A GCSE grade C or above (or equivalent) in Mathematics and English.	2 years.	Application deadlines are on their website.	Go to the Teach First website.	This programme is designed not just to provide teacher training but also transferrable leadership skills. They ask for 'exceptional graduates' and train them to become 'inspiring teachers and leaders'. Students will receive an unqualified teacher's salary for the first year and possibly a Newly Qualified Teacher's (NQT's) salary for the second year. In August 2010, this programme was restricted to certain schools, but the aim is to introduce the scheme to more areas.

Type of ITT course	Qualifications required	Length of course (based on full-time study)	When to apply	How to apply	Other comments
Assessment-based training	• Degree at a pass level and a substantial amount of teaching experience based in a UK school.	Up to a year.	Any time.	Through the University of Gloucestershire School of Education, the administrators.	You will need to compile a portfolio containing evidence of your ability to teach. There is a day-long assessment visit to your school. Not available in Wales.

Appendix 2
An example of a lesson plan

Outcomes: To be able to list the parts of the digestive system and trace the path of the food through it.

Time	Activity	V, A or K?	Assessment method
0–6	Writing objectives, settling down.		
7–10	Discussion – what did you eat at lunch? Where is it now? Point to that part on your body.	A, K	Observe where they're pointing.
11–20	Show them the model digestive system, getting them to point on their body where the oesophagus, stomach, small and large intestine are.	V, A, K	Observe where they're pointing.
21–27	Show them the video clips of what the stomach and small intestine look like.	V	
28–40	Writing their own mnemonic to list the order of the parts of the digestive system. Judge them at the end and get the class to vote for a winner.	K	Judging.
41–48	In groups, hold a competition for them to hold up the cards of the parts of the digestive system in the correct order.	K	Watch for the order and look for misconceptions or misunderstandings.
49–50	Packing away.		

Resources: model of digestive system

Differentiation: EH has a visual impairment, so is sitting at the front of the room; HI may need to sit down during the card activity – TA will allow for this; TA to circulate around the rest of the students when no physical movement is required to help check for misconceptions, especially with DR and MH – also to make sure GR is able to read all of the key words.

Evaluation:

Appendix 3
An example of a behaviour contract

Adapted from Rogers (1998)

Behaviour contract for:

Date:

I have discussed my behaviour with the following people:

_____

_____

_____

_____

and have agreed to work with them in changing my behaviour.

Behaviours I have agreed to work on:

_____

_____

_____

_____

How will I do it?

_____

_____

_____

_____

How my teacher will support me:

_____

_____

_____

_____

Comments on the pupil's progress.

Week 1

_____

_____

_____

_____

Week 2

_____

_____

_____

_____

Week 3

_____

_____

_____

_____

Week 4

_____

_____

_____

_____

Reward from school if my behaviour improves:

_____

_____

_____

_____

Reward from home if my behaviour at school improves:

_____

_____

_____

_____

Signed (pupil)

Signed (teacher)

Signed (parent)

Appendix 4
Brilliant websites

Part 1: Starting Out

Direct.gov	*For current available funding*	http://www.direct.gov.uk
Every Child Matters		http://www.dcsf.gov.uk/everychildmatters/
Graduate Teacher Training Registry (GTTR)	*For applying for postgraduate training courses*	http://www.gttr.ac.uk
National Strategies		http://nationalstrategies.standards.dcsf.gov.uk/
Ofsted	*For up-to-date reports on schools*	http://www.ofsted.gov.uk/Ofsted-home/Inspection-reports
Standards Site	*For familiarising yourself with the National Curriculum*	http://www.standards.dfes.gov.uk/schemes3/
Teach First	*For more information about the 'Teach First' course*	http://www.teachfirst.org.uk/
Teaching in Scotland		http://www.teachinginscotland.com/
Times Educational Supplement (TES Connect)	*For checking current salaries*	http://www.tes.co.uk
Training and Development Agency for Schools	*For comparing courses and finding course providers*	http://www.tda.gov.uk

Part 1: Starting Out

	For practising QTS skills tests	http://www.tda.gov.uk/skillstests/numeracy/practicematerials.aspx
		http://www.tda.gov.uk/skillstests/literacy/practicematerials.aspx
		http://www.tda.gov.uk/skillstests/ict/practicematerials.aspx
	For the Student Associates Scheme	http://www.tda.gov.uk/Recruit/experienceteaching/jointhestudentassociatesscheme.aspx
	For viewing the Professional Standards	http://www.tda.gov.uk/teacher/developing-career/professional-standards-guidance.aspx
UK National Academic Recognition Information Centre	For checking the equivalence of qualifications gained abroad	http://www.naric.org.uk/
Universities and Colleges Admissions Service (UCAS)	For applying for undergraduate and postgraduate courses	http://www.ucas.ac.uk
University of Gloucestershire School of Education	For Assessment-based training	http://www.glos.ac.uk

Part 3: Ideas for Delivering High-Quality Lessons

VAK Learning	For assessing learning styles	http://www.brainboxx.co.uk/A3_ASPECTS/pages/VAK_quest.htm
		http://www.ldpride.net/learning-style-test-b.html
Assessment for Learning		
Qualifications and Curriculum Development Agency (QCDA)	For formal assessment, including APP	http://www.qcda.gov.uk/26.aspx
Goal on-line	Online assessment programme	http://www.goalonline.co.uk/
Many of the links in the 'E-learning' section below are also relevant		
E-learning		
BBC	For video clips	http://www.bbc.co.uk
	For online tests and interactive animations	http://www.bbc.co.uk/schools/bitesize
Brainpop	For animations	http://www.brainpop.com/
Classtools	For the random name selector and other assessment for learning tools	http://classtools.net
Interwrite	Interactive Whiteboard Software	http://www.gtcocalcomp.com/interwritesoftware_schools.htm
Quizbusters	For 'Blockbusters' style online games, linked to the National Curriculum and syllabi	http://www.teachers-direct.co.uk/resources/quiz-busters/quiz-busters-directory.aspx

Part 3: Ideas for Delivering High-Quality Lessons

E-learning		
Quizdom	For electronic voting pads	http://www.qwizdom.co.uk
S-cool	For GCSE and A-Level revision	http://www.s-cool.co.uk/
Schoolsnet	For interactive revision	http://www.schoolsnet.com
Skoool	For interactive animations at the secondary level	http://www.skoool.co.uk
SMART Notebook	Interactive Whiteboard Software	http://smarttech.com/
Snagit	A tool for capturing pictures and video from your desktop	http://TechSmith.com/Snagit
TES	For resources made by other teachers	http://www.tes.co.uk/resources
Being observed		
TDA	For viewing the Professional Standards	http://www.tda.gov.uk/teacher/developing-career/professional-standards-guidance.aspx

Part 5: Looking Ahead		
Applying for jobs		
Ofsted	*To find the most recent report on a school*	http://www.ofsted.gov.uk/Ofsted-home/Inspection-reports
Schools Recruitment Service	*For finding teaching jobs*	https://www.schoolsrecruitment.dcsf.gov.uk/
TDA	*For advice on looking for jobs, including links to websites*	http://www.tda.gov.uk/Recruit/becomingateacher/lookingforajob.aspx
Teachernet	*For advice on looking for jobs and links to recruitment websites*	http://www.teachernet.gov.uk/professionaldevelopment/careers/vacancies/
TES	*For finding teaching jobs*	http://www.tes.co.uk
Conclusion: Staying sane		
TDA	*For a list of teaching unions*	http://www.teachernet.gov.uk/professionaldevelopment/professionalassociations/unions/

Appendix 5
Brilliant further reading

Adams, H. and Nadel, I. (Ed) (2008) *The Education of Henry Adams (Oxford World's Classics)*, Oxford Paperbacks.

Passing the skills tests:

Ferrigan, C. (2008) *Passing the ICT Skills Test (Achieving QTS)*, 3rd edition, Learning Matters Ltd, Exeter.

Johnson, J. (2008) *Passing the Literacy Skills Test (Achieving QTS)*, 2nd edition, Learning Matters Ltd, Exeter.

Patmore, M. (2008) *Passing the Numeracy Skills Test (Achieving QTS)*, 4th edition, Learning Matters Ltd, Exeter.

For the paper about the University of Plymouth's doodling research:

Andrade, J. (2010) What does doodling do? *Applied Cognitive Psychology*, 24: 100–106. doi: 10.1002/acp.1561.

For some background on Assessment for Learning:

Black, P., Harrison, C., Lee, C., Marshall, B. and William, D. (2004) *Working Inside the Black Box: Assessment for Learning in the Classroom*, NFER Nelson.

For further advice on differentiation and learning styles:

Marzano, R.J. and Kendall, J.S. (Eds) (2007) *The New Taxonomy of Educational Objectives*, 2nd edition, Corwin Press.

Sprenger, M. (2008). *Differentiation Through Learning Styles and Memory*, 2nd edition, Corwin Press.

For advice on behaviour management:

Rogers, W.A. (1998) *You Know the Fair Rule: Strategies for Making the Hard Job of Discipline in Schools Easier*, 2nd edition, Financial Times/ Prentice Hall.

For more information about using NLP to help build relationships:

O'Connor, J. and Seymour, J. (2003) *Introducing NLP Neuro-Linguistic Programming: Psychological Skills for Understanding and Influencing People*, revised 2nd edition, Thorsons.

To keep up to date with teaching issues:

The Times Educational Supplement (weekly newspaper).

For the research by Sanders and Rivers:

Sanders, W.L. and Rivers J.C. (1996) *Cumulative and Residual Effects of Teachers on Future Student Academic Achievement*, University of Tennessee Value – Added Research and Assessment Centre, Knoxville.

Appendix 6
Acronyms

APP – Assessing Pupils' Progress

AfL – Assessment for Learning

AST – Advanced Skills Teacher

BA – Bachelor of Arts (degree)

BSc – Bachelor of Science (degree)

BTEC – British and Technology Education Council (qualification)

CATs – Cognitive Ability Tests or Credit and Accumulation Transfer Scheme (e.g. CATS points)

CRB – Criminal Records Bureau

DCSF – Department for Children, Schools and Families

EBD – Emotional and Behavioural Difficulties

EBITT – Employment Based Initial Teacher Training

GCSE – General Certificate of Secondary Education

GTP – Graduate Teacher Programme

GTTR – Graduate Teacher Training Registry

HND – Higher National Diploma

ICT – Information and Communication Technology

IEP – Individual Education Plan

ITT – Initial Teacher Training

LEA – Local Education Authority

MTL – Masters in Teaching and Learning

NCA – National Curriculum Assessment

NLP – Neuro-linguistic Programming

NQT – Newly Qualified Teacher

Ofsted – Office for Standards in Education

PGCE – Post Graduate Certificate in Education or Professional Graduate Certificate in Education

QCDA – Qualifications and Curriculum Development Agency

QTS – Qualified Teacher Status

RTP – Registered Teacher Programme

SAS – Student Associates Scheme

SAT – Standard Attainment Tests

SCITT – School-centred Initial Teacher Training

SEN – Special Educational Needs

SENCo – Special Educational Needs Coordinator

SLT – Senior Leadership Team

SMT – Senior Management Team

TA – Teaching Assistant

TDA – Training and Development Agency for Schools

TES – Times Educational Supplement

UCAS – Universities and Colleges Admissions Service

UK NARIC – UK National Academic Recognition Information Centre

VAK – Visual, Auditory and Kinaesthetic

VLE – Virtual Learning Environment

Index